£. 7.99

'A remarkably readable and compelling book, offering much of value, at many levels. Michael Blastland, an erudite, incisive, thoughtful and articulate BBC producer, has provided us with an entertaining and educational account of life with Joe, his ten-year-old prototypical, severely autistic son. Read it. Enjoy it. Learn from it. It will haunt you.'
Bernard Rimland, PhD, director of the Autism Research Institute, founder of the Autism Society of America, technical consultant for *Rain Man*

'A moving story ... Blastland has performed a remarkable service in baring his family life for us.' Simon Baron-Cohen, *Guardian*

'Deeply personal and moving ... Blastland's beautifully written book offers us a glimpse of the torments endured by the growing number of children born with their cerebral pathways wrongly wired.'
Val Hennessy, *Daily Mail*

'From this careful, serious book emerges a man with a quick wit and far-seeing eye for what makes life so peculiar ... [Joe] stands out as a work of rare enlightenment' Melissa Katsoulis, *Sunday Telegraph*

'[Blastland's] honesty is in keeping with a compelling, brave and highly readable book that never verges on the sentimental.'
Julie Wheelwright, *Independent*

**MICHAEL BLASTLAND** lives in a small village in Hertfordshire, often with his daughter Cait, less often and more noisily with his son Joe. A journalist all his professional life, he started on weekly newspapers before moving to the BBC where he makes programmes for Radio 4, including *Analysis* and *More or Less*.

# Joe

## The only boy in the world

MICHAEL BLASTLAND

**P**

PROFILE BOOKS

This paperback edition published in 2007

First published in Great Britain in 2006 by
PROFILE BOOKS LTD
3A Exmouth House
Pine Street
Exmouth Market
London EC1R 0JH
www.profilebooks.com

10 9 8 7 6 5 4 3 2 1

Typeset in Goudy Old Style by MacGuru Ltd
info@macguru.org.uk

Printed and bound in Great Britain by
Bookmarque Ltd, Croydon, Surrey

A CIP catalogue record for this book is available from the British Library.

ISBN-10 1 86197 944 4
ISBN-13 978 1 86197 944 5

For Joe and Cait

# Contents

1 Fascination                                    1
2 Experience                                     9
3 Obsession                                     26
4 Language                                      56
5 Intention                                     80
6 Self-consciousness                           111
7 Storytelling                                  123
8 Innocence                                     144
9 Seeing                                        164
10 Meaning                                      182
   Postscript                                   195
   Epilogue: Autumn 2006                        206

   *Acknowledgements*                           209
   *Further Reading*                            212

# 1
# Fascination

This book is about a boy called Joe. He's ten and he's my son. It's a story of strange happenings and human riddles, it invites fantastical speculation and argues something brazen, preposterous even: that until you know Joe's unusual life, you won't fully understand your own.

Joe is a brown-haired, freckle-faced imp struck with an unusual variety of mental disability that leaves him at once vulnerable, charming and tyrannical. He digs his nails into your deepest sensibilities much as he digs them under your skin, wrenches you this way and that, and then, reaching his hand into yours or folding like a deckchair into a clatter of laughter, disarms you with innocence.

Ostensibly, he has little to say to the rest of us. He shares few of our pleasures, has many perplexing eccentricities and isn't someone you'd instinctively turn to for enlightenment. Not quite the philosopher king, then. Joe is packed with strange urges and passions, missing many normal motivations and unable to make sense of the world in ways the rest of us take for granted – an odd one, to be sure. By and large such oddness is kept out of sight, tucked away in special schools or behind the shy doors of suburban semis where all too often families become isolated by love and the duty of care; that or the simple awkwardness of getting out and about with strangeness in tow.

Joe is now in a special school too, brought here into public view. I make no apology for throwing so much attention at him because with luck the result will be better understanding in two directions: ours of him, and ours of ourselves. Sadly, it might never run in the obvious third direction: quite probably he will never understand other people.

He started school in late August 2004. A small part of what follows is an account of the turbulent months surrounding that event. More riotously, the book relates some of the many moving and absurd episodes in his life that led us to the borders of madness, before which we never could have let him go; more recklessly, it uses my son's history to investigate what makes the rest of us tick.

Joe was born with a perfect knot in his umbilical cord. Somehow, turning somersaults in the womb, he threaded himself through a loop in his own lifeline. There was a time when we thought this might explain his disability, but in all likelihood the knot had nothing to do with it, for there's no damage to Joe's brain of the kind that shows up in a scan as a result of oxygen starvation; no palsy. The only, and I have to say unconvincing, explanation was that his thoughts misfire owing to an entirely different, metabolic, cause – something to do with two of the amino acids that help make up the chemical soup in his brain. Nowadays he lives with the label 'autistic': broad, ill-defined, ill-fitting and unexplained, a label that's best put aside before getting to know him. But for me at least, and perhaps others who know his story, the loop in the cord became a metaphor: it framed a passage for Joe into an altogether alien existence that is magical, mysterious and infuriating in equal measure. When he tumbled into that oblique version of life, it was through the looking glass, through the doors of an enchanted wardrobe, while behind him the exit shut tight.

So unlike the birth of our first child, Cait, a dream of music and ease and elation, Joe's arrival was frightening, the hospital disorganised, the breech birth undiagnosed, the pain-relief elusive until scandalously late. As Joe made his assisted way out, his pattering pulse ran into the sand and it was then that I noticed the room was stuffed with people. Joe's foot was first to arrive: absurd, limp and bluish. Some cumbersome minutes later, but within seconds of his head and the swift snip of that cord, a man in a white coat scooped him to one side, gave him injections, worked silently, attentively, and cajoled the breath into him. So slow, so lazy was Joe's embrace of life that we used to say it took a couple of months for him to agree that life was what he wanted.

In the years since Joe's looking-glass moment, however it happened, his differences have always been mesmerising to me, but I've been, in a peculiar way, selfish with them. Part of the blame for my wanting to share them now lies with the historian Felipe Fernandez-Armesto, who forced me to declare my first ramshackle reflections, though I absolve him, naturally, of any responsibility for their content. Felipe and I bumped into each other one day outside my editor's office at the BBC. Bumping into him is the one sure way of jolting Felipe into recognition, as his wife will testify.

'Ah, Michael!' he began, with typical ebullience. 'How are you?' Then, with the same tone and chirpiness: 'And how's your boy?'

I told him the latest. His smile barely faded; his prompt reply took me aback: 'Fascinating! Fascinating!'

Fascinating? I'd been used to concern, appreciative understanding; used to sympathy, pity, remorse – not eager intellectual *amusement*. My much-cultivated sangfroid was altogether jumping in my veins at the thought. 'Fascinating?' As I realised instantly, but years late, Felipe was right, and in that unblinking moment I became dimly aware that it was possibly the most consoling thing I'd ever heard, and felt as though Joe sat high on my shoulders.

Fascinating. I'd long been fascinated by Joe, but I had reason. Now I was encouraged to think, as I had never quite before, that it wasn't only a selfish fascination, that of course Joe is one of the most fascinating among us. Quirky, maddening, hilarious, adorable, hateful, sensitive, dangerous and exposed; he goes through his life's repertoire on a fairground waltzer. *Of course* he deserves our attention, and when we give it, what things he tells us, what questions he asks.

As I tap these words onto a screen, Joe is upstairs sitting in bed during a holiday at home, chirping much later into the night than he ought. Today, an unexceptional day, he made a notable discovery: Daddy's name can be spoken without strenuous effort a steady ten times a minute or more for what feels like a good hour and the effect is to send Daddy progressively bananas. That is, Joe *would* have learnt as much from this behaviour, *if* he learnt. The fact is that in general he doesn't learn, or at least does so inch by painful inch, but the reason he doesn't has a surprising way of showing us how we do – the different ways he has of seeing the world encourage us to re-examine our own.

The events in his life are sometimes mortifying, sometimes comical, poignant or weird, but above all for me now, they are fascinating. Fascination is one of the great consolations of this life of his, otherwise so frustrating, and I prefer that kind of consolation to pity; but thinking about Joe's uniqueness pays doubly, with a deeper understanding of all our humanity than I could ever achieve by dwelling on my own.

What makes him fascinating? In part, seeing what we have in comparison to what he lacks. He makes much that we take for granted appear suddenly luminous, and we see equally starkly where we would be without it. As one eminent researcher put it, Joe's condition teaches us 'nothing less than the people-ness of people'.

Has he, then, become no more than an edifying puzzle? Not, I think, when his arms wrap around my neck with enough vice-like eagerness to mince vertebrae, when his voice chimes meaninglessly in selfless happiness with the pure clarity of bird-song, or when confusion and frustration muddy his handsome face, and I'm reminded that there can be no greater puzzle than the way we appear to him. At all times, as well as offering the rest of us fascination, he has a habit of continuing on his own sweet way without regard for what anyone thinks, a habit of continuing to be himself, oblivious to whether he's fascinating or not.

I call him the only boy in the world because this is quite likely how it seems to him, living as he does without many of the commonplace nuts and bolts of ordinary human perception and understanding, in the absence of which he can never know even the elementary facts that he has kin and kind. That is, I *think* that is how it seems to him, because much is speculation, even among the experts, and Joe is in no position to put us right. And it has to be said that what I write may be true only of Joe and entirely at odds with the perceptions and experience of others on the autistic spectrum.

But the evidence, even if unique, is often compelling. The stories in these pages came about because Joe doesn't do what most of us do, and do often without thinking, except when we're nudged into reflection by seeing what goes wrong in those who aren't so instinctively astute. While we manoeuvre through the fantastic complexity of ordinary living, managing to navigate human society with all its rules, rituals and expectations, Joe careers by in a circus clown's exploding banger. If you observe his scrapes and confusions, you can't help wondering how easy it is to go wrong and about the remarkable talents that mostly preserve the rest of us from disaster. What are these talents? How do we do it? Joe, by a kind of reverse engineering, helps to show us.

What we see when peering into his mental machinery is a

child possibly lacking almost all the philosopher's traditional definitions of what it is to be human. There is a list which varies a little but usually includes a high degree of self-awareness, sophisticated culture, rich use of technology or tool-making, a sense of our own history, structured language, an advanced ability to reason, complex moralities, the ability to think in abstraction or metaphor, and so on. I know the academic distinctions, I've read arguments from philosophy, neuroscience and elsewhere about what makes our species unique, or not. If I follow these distinctions, if I accept their logic, I'm forced to a rueful conclusion: Joe, my son, doesn't qualify. If they are right about the attributes essential to being human, then I must face that chilling verdict. It is an outrageous question for a father to address, whether his child is one of us, but by suggesting that we can learn from him through the many ways he sets the rest of us in such sharp relief, I invite that question. How different can you be, how many fundamentals can you lack, and still be human? My head gives my heart some trouble on this, and though there can be no suspense about which side I favour in the end, I hope to reconcile head and heart in the following chapters. Part of what I hope Joe also shows us through these stories, once we see where the differences and similarities lie, is which are the ones that matter.

I remember when the decision about his immediate future weighed most heavily. 'No point,' one well-wisher said, 'ruining your own life for someone whose life is already ruined.' He was a kind man, a good man, who meant well and intended to console me, but the word burned. Ruined. I pictured a cartoon caricature of physical dereliction: a crumbling castle wearing Joe's glummest face: roofless, remote, desolate in the tumbleweed. Was my son's life a ruin – redundant and pointless? The thought revolts me, but say it is true? Say there is no hope?

All right, I reply, so ruins have no future and might be inhospitable, but more than any home comfort they incomparably fire the imagination, and so, even if for that reason alone, repay all the attention we can muster. Of course, I want better for Joe than that. This book has become my attempt to hoist him into view, not just as inspiration to the rest of us but as so much more besides. I hope it does justice to the confused, exuberant pinball that is Joe. I also hope you will find it a fine place for your imagination, that something here will leave you either fascinated by him or startled at yourself.

# 2
# Experience

'If you get lost,' they said, 'follow the signs to the zoo.'

'Ha! Joe is going to live in the zoo,' we laugh, as we pass signposts of elephants pointing the way, and silently share a more sombre thought: is he? It's the summer of 2004 and Joe is due to be assessed for a place at a special residential school. He's nine years old.

... And I think back to another day, in spring, at about eight o'clock, when Joe's sister Cait was hustled out to the car for the morning rush and the front door closed on a still and silent house, all haste and muddle of the morning packed and bundled outside, Joe left behind.

Joe's prospective new school, as it comes into view on the road past the Downs, is a row of aloof Victorian houses, beautifully set, not far from the river Avon at Clifton, Brunel's suspension bridge atop the gorge as if to frame it, to please the eye more than shift traffic. We face an hour or two of meetings and a tour of the school to settle two questions: are they willing to have him and do we want him to go? The second is proving hardest. Other schools have places – all, like this one, far from home; all inadvertently feeding not calming our disquiet.

Perhaps this will be different. I hope so, we're running out of options.

... And I think again of that morning when Joe lay upstairs in bed, apparently asleep. I imagine his peaceful breathing and how, once awake, he'd stretch and lie singing an aimless melody, getting up only when he needed to. Seldom would he do anything without the whole house knowing.

If all goes well at this school, if we like them and they like him, he will live here for the next nine years, 120 miles from us. I feel it as an exile, a punishment for Joe, who scarcely knows what's happening to him or why. A punishment for what?

... I think of how ordinary a morning it was, the day more than any other that precipitated this, and how ordinarily he would charge into another room in the morning to wrestle his way under the covers with someone already awake, or soon woken, so he could begin the game we know as 'Beds'. 'Beds', according to rules for the pathologically fastidious, is played as follows: the duvet must precisely and squarely cover each corner, Joe's soft toys must be gathered like colourful tramps in a doss house – a Teletubby or two, Postman Pat, Winnie the Pooh – stuffed in with the parent, tucked up to the chin. Everything must be just so. Next, the pillows must be repositioned according to some rule I've never understood, and then if the curtains are open they must be drawn, after which we're required to spend a few moments under the duvet whispering the word 'dark' before emerging to realign it at the corners. Finally, the whole arrangement must be turned through 90 or 180 degrees on the bed before we start all over again. Participation is usually compulsory. But not that day. It was a morning when Joe seemed to be slumbering, while Geraldine, the French au pair and one of Joe's most capable carers, yawned in her room, the door ajar for her to catch the sound should he stir.

If all goes well, they'll see his potential, find his behaviour manageable and see the fascinating, often likeable child; nothing will be smashed, no one hit, he won't scream (too much), he'll be Jekyll, not Hyde.

… And I think – how he wouldn't have trod lightly that other morning. He runs – you can just about call it that – stiff legged and thudding, on heels more than toes, so that you'd hardly label him surreptitious. That spring day he got up and made his way downstairs unseen and unheard.

If all goes well, we'll know in a day or two if the routine of nine years is over, years in which I've increasingly stared at Joe wondering how the world looks from there, why the wiring in his head doesn't seem to connect the way it connects in us, wondering if by understanding the points of difference between him and the rest of us I can find a way to fix them. Watching him now, I see he's edgy, almost afraid of this foreign place and mistrusting the day's sense of occasion, what with everyone strangely together.

… I remember how at that other time the front door had a chain attached with Joe in mind. Having mastered the Yale lock some time ago, he'd rattled that chain many times, knowing it to be the last obstacle to escape. That morning, being so swiftly on the tail of his mother and sister, Joe found the chain not yet in place, turned the doorknob, pulled, and was out, where the trees on the hill were in hopeful blossom. Mum's red car must have turned the corner at the end of the street a few seconds earlier.

We turn away from the Downs into the drive, lined with trees now hoarding the darkening green of summer, pull up in the car park at the back and climb out. I look around, feeling for the mood of the place, if one can be felt, trying to learn Joe's fate from the atmosphere. And if he hates it, and if they find him too much of a handful?

… And I think, that it was always possible that something like the events of that other morning would happen, given Joe's form for doing a runner. The first time he slipped his guard was outside the infants' school where he'd been dragged as usual one afternoon to collect Cait. Usually then obedient enough to stand and wait, Joe melted away in the mêlée of children charging through the school gate and set off with purpose. He was five years old and already possessed sufficient sense of direction to find his way to a house he'd visited maybe once or twice in his life, where a schoolfriend of his sister lived. He was found, across two roads, knocking on the door some ten minutes later when the schoolfriend arrived home with her mother.

What if they find him too much, as we have begun to find him too much? Not just odd but with a bubbling, insistent kind of oddity that would overflow into something alarming and beyond our ability to cope. That's what brought us to Bristol, when the coping slipped on that spring morning, the day that led to this. No one was to blame, it was just oddity asserting itself, finally, in a way that made us realise we had been at the limits too long. Joe has one hand in mine and the other grasping my sleeve. Does he know? His fear suggests so.

… And then I remember the second great getaway, on holiday, when by taking a sudden turn he shook off his grandparents who were escorting him back from the beach to their rented cottage. After a long and increasingly frantic search he was found in a garden shed. Most infants and small toddlers are connected to their parents by an instinctive thread that stretches no more than 100 feet or so. Leave them to crawl or wander freely and they rarely go further. Ever since he's been able to get about, Joe has been drawn to the distant horizon, showing no fear.

He's clinging to his mother now as we make our way inside, and we're coaxing him into the cooler shadows, first to reception and then to the large room with the high ceiling and a circle of chairs. We're invited to sit and wait. To calm him, we ask him to count the growing number of strangers facing us.

'How many people, Joe?'

'Ine, oo, ee, bor, by, ix …'

… And I think of his first full breakout, more than a sudden dash for freedom this time; a full-blown escape – the time we realised he'd worked out how to spring the latch on the front door. He fumbled his way by trial and error into the open, plodded along the road a short way to another house he'd also visited maybe once before and was found a couple of minutes later knocking like a metronome, wearing nothing but his underpants. He popped into the same house again a few weeks later, finding his own front door more secure now thanks to the recent addition of that chain, but discovering a second route to the street through the back garden and via the garage. It was becoming habitual, like prisoners escaping Stalag Luft III. No matter that we tried to Joe-proof the exits, he would find a way out. I awaited the discovery of a tunnel under the kitchen boiler. On his third breakout, he had barged past the woman at number 22 before he was caught. 'He's already got a video in his hand,' she said. 'Can't you let him watch it?' He seemed happy enough after all.

Happy? Yes, you could say that. This was what lured him out: the knowledge that in other people's houses lurked children's videos – his keenest desire and, banned at home in an effort to control his fixation, his most heartfelt torment; a vicious addiction that drove him like a heroin user into ever more frenzied hunger, and escape.

And so it was that he emerged on that clear spring morning, Mummy gone to school with Cait, the unchained door no bar to his infatuation, leaving him free from physical restraint but with compulsion chattering in his ear, making getaway number six, his last.

I imagine him thinking as the latch yielded that this was the day he'd been waiting for; a clear-blue, beautiful opportunity, no adult to bridle him, no barriers, no inhibitions, as in bare feet and wearing only his trademark blue Y-fronts he sees a neighbour's open front door. It's not his usual bolt hole but a different house this time, one across the street.

The delicious promise of a glimpsed living room is that it will grant him a fix, a shot of that one thing most compelling, which in his life is *Postman Pat*, *101 Dalmatians*, *Wallace and Gromit*, *Aladdin*, or who knows what variety of heaven. For a while, if you failed to catch him, he'd punctuate every walk along a suburban street with furtive lunges down garden paths, rapping on doors, ringing bells.

Head down, jagged limbs threshing across the pavement, the front door of his own house left open, he was out, into the traffic.

Inside the car trundling down the hill between close-parked cars, the young driver not long into his licence was helpless as a near-naked, pale-skinned figure appeared in front of his bonnet. There was the screech of tyres and a raw metallic thud, said a neighbour afterwards, a flash of dark brown hair and a boy flung past the windscreen and over the other side. The car wrenched itself still.

Joe had tumbled into the road. He hit the tarmac. I suppose you might say he was lucky. He landed feet first and somehow remained upright, planted like a chess piece – a small miracle. Scorning impossibility now, he quickly reoriented himself. I've no doubt it hurt – how could it not hurt to be hit by a car, sent spinning over the bonnet then dumped over the side? But why interrupt his destiny? He trotted off with the same careless determination for the same destination and with no more perhaps than a few of his what I call curses, angry grunts, like rugby players connecting at a scrum.

'Ang!' he says.

'Ang!'

No one knew how – we shook our heads in disbelief – but

we discovered later that there wasn't a mark on him. Fate plays its fickle game at the extremes with Joe, at once damning and charming. Still at speed, relatively, he toddled down the path and through the open door into the stranger's house, surveyed his surroundings, recognised the front room as the type most likely to yield that idiosyncratic black jewel, his plastic booty, spotted the TV, scanned the spines of the videos next to it and snatched at one. Frantic with illicit expectation, he'd have fumbled open the case and stuffed the rectangular box into the slot, pressed play – no developmental delay in evidence there – and stepped back. I picture him as the titles roll, wild-eyed, rocking backwards and forwards from one foot to the other, arms fluttering, yelping, pointing, full of delirious excitement and all the while regarded with what can only have been utter bewilderment by the house's young occupant about to be late for work.

'Well, you see, there was this boy, and …'

How often, after all, do strangers' eight-year-olds pop by for a video all but naked? Convict-like, but with disarming lack of self-consciousness, he'd pitched up in the morning rush and helped himself; manners, ceremony, inhibition, privacy, property … all meaningless to this bizarre, chirping, baffling intruder. For Joe, it had been a most satisfactory and stimulating start to the day.

Joe is fiercely motivated and often blithely uninhibited: propelled by obsession but careless, he's an untethered party balloon in a gale. By and large, other passing cars had been until then merely a palette of noisy colours, rumbling down the hill.

We'd stand and watch them sometimes, with Joe calling out as they went by, as near as he could to red, blue, green and white: 'Ed!' 'Boo!' 'Een!' 'Ite!' He knew nothing of the danger they presented, and until that moment had shown them no fear.

My guess is that Joe has always suffered from a poverty of experience, an excessive selectivity which means he neither can, nor cares to, dip into the rest of life's data swimming busily about him. He draws from a statistical sample of one: himself. We all favour this kind of evidence, finding on the whole our own experience to be our best guide, but tend not to grant it quite such exclusivity. The rest of us know that things could be other than the way they were for us. We amass this knowledge from other sources: other people, books, TV, our own imaginations. Joe, finding other people a mystery, their minds impenetrable, is slow to pick up what has been ours, and so attends inordinately to what's been his. Thus his entire knowledge of cars was that they either transported him or slid by.

The problem comes about not because Joe is unable to communicate or because he is so intellectually impaired that nothing makes sense to him; I can have something like a conversation with him even though speech is among the weakest of his skills. I can tell him facts – that the shop is closed, that the pasta is all gone – and he will understand, but these are facts about material things. His difficulty is with inner facts, the facts of human experience. Joe seems to live within himself to a degree that even the most private among us would find hard to imagine. I don't mean that he is unaffectionate or shuns people who are close to him, he can be the most tactile child, happy on occasion to soak selected strangers in kisses whether they like it or not; it is rather a mental isolation, a solitariness of consciousness whereby he fails to learn that other lives are lived too, fails to appreciate that we all exist in a state of subjectivity, all have points of view; fails, in short, to think of other people as other people. This is what leads him to reject so much of the experience that could help him: he just doesn't see its relevance; worse, he seems not even to know it's there, and so cannot begin to do what the rest of us do compulsively and share experience. Hence the fanatical devotion to what he already knows, for after all, as far as he's concerned, it's all there is, or at least all that matters. This includes his attitude to videos, food, toys, where only the familiar will do, and also, to take the example to hand, what to be afraid of.

Walking round the school in Bristol or sitting in its meeting room among strangers, he wants to go home. It's not normal, this earnest focus of adult attention from so many, this coming to a place which holds no pleasure for him. What is it about fear that infects him now, but not then?

Fear strikes us as instinctive, an elementary passion, a rush of adrenalin. We've all heard of the fight-and-flight mechanism, the hard-wired trigger in the brain that supposedly governs our response to any threat, but we can exaggerate the biological basis of fear. Joe's problem here is not that he doesn't know what fear is. Whatever the slice of grey matter that tells the heart to quiver, the eyes to stretch and the muscles to tense is in perfect working order in Joe. He's afraid of cars now, all right. There's nothing wrong with his fight-or-flight mechanism these two years hence and that's not because the accident rewired his brain where it was wrongly wired before. The problem is that he doesn't instinctively know what to be afraid of, and nor does anyone else. There's nothing in our genes to tell us that unattended luggage is scary. Fear has to be in part socially constructed, it has to be learnt; other people have to tell us to some extent what to be afraid of. That should be obvious enough, for unless we know what a fast-moving car can do, what a gun is, how American foreign policy is motivated and what its likely consequences, why should we fear them?

A chimpanzee raised in a zoo has no fear of snakes. One raised in the wild seems to learn from the anxiety of others who are older or more experienced to keep away, and soon starts to pass on the same clamorous warning. A chimp in a zoo, ignorant of the danger of snakes, once introduced to a chimp from the wild, is quick to learn the routine. Their fear is contagious. This is conclusive evidence, say certain primatologists, that chimps have culture in the same way humans do. If it were true that they were creatures only of instinct, one would expect fear and alarm of this kind to be either universal among them or non-existent. It's neither: chimps have to learn fear from each other. Thus we get to the nub of Joe's difficulty in this respect: being so cumbersomely slow at picking up cultural or social clues, of broadening his experience with the help of others, gives him the appearance of being eccentrically despotic in his own attitude to the world, of being in the broadest sense uncultured.

The advantages of being able to communicate danger are

obvious. It saves each one of us having to discover what it means first hand by possibly fatal experience. If you don't know the harm a snake can do until its bite takes poisonous effect, your education has arrived late. If you don't know the harm a car can do until it sends you skyward, the learning curve might be too steep to survive. Such cultural knowledge is invaluable, if it can be passed on in advance.

'Cars, danger Joe.'

'Car,' he says.

'Cars ouch!'

'Car.'

'Car bang! Joe ouch!' With a thump on the carpet for effect.

And he laughs.

No matter how often it was said in how many ways, no matter what games with toys, Joe picked up less cultural understanding of this danger than the chimps of theirs. Until his accident he paid traffic little regard, happily ambling down the middle of roads.

Cultural knowledge can't exist without the ability to pass it on. It was once said to be uniquely human. It is not, though it certainly makes human society possible, shared experience being a reservoir of education, a reservoir Joe can barely sip from.

At the new school, by being asked to perform his reading or typing skills for teachers, being required to sit in an unfamiliar room under the gaze of others, Joe probably recognises this as a place of unwelcome compulsion to broaden his experience, make him learn and do new things. He's been at a school before and the paraphernalia of certain kinds of books, tables, pencils and paper will be worryingly suggestive. What he sees this day that's recognisable is unwelcome, and what he sees of strange people in a strange place is unwelcome simply for being strange. He's confronted with a mixture of the new and the disliked, not a happy combination. Experience counsels escape on both counts.

On the roadside in the small town where Joe lives, cars had never previously included among their very familiar characteristics of noise, movement and colour, the extra quality of causing pain. The poor young driver, who knew this characteristic well enough to hit the brakes and had now sensed it with an immediacy he never expected, was in a terrible state. He phoned his father on his mobile, unable or unwilling to get back behind the wheel. In time, the police arrived, then an ambulance. Social services were notified. Geraldine, the au pair, had drifted back to sleep and didn't hear a tentative knock on the front door. No one could get any sense from the manic, happy boy in the underpants in front of the video, whose only response to the police was that, look, it's Pat.

They concluded – wrongly – that the child had been left to fend for himself, so he had. I remember picturing the headline: 'Home Alone Dice With Death ... Disabled Boy Abandoned'.

Joe is wary of traffic now, steps gingerly into the road with nervous looks and takes to the pavement in haste, but he had to feel pain and shock personally, directly, to learn that cars could cause them. More fundamentally, though he understands what pain and injury are, I'm not sure if he will ever conceive of that ultimate injury, death. Other children begin with the idea of death as an extension of sleep, and don't fully understand it as a permanent loss of consciousness until they're five or older. Until then, developmental psychologists report, children seem to think that thoughts persist in the dead in some form. Even so, they understand well enough at a very early age that death is a condition with little to recommend it. At Joe's rate of learning, he might be very old indeed, with the kind of experience to inform him that I'd rather not contemplate, before the idea makes any sense at all. Whereas others will become fond, aged four or thereabouts, of asking about the magnitude of any danger – 'Will it kill me?' – imperfect though their understanding of death must be, Joe might never ask, for he has never heard of it.

All of which is some disadvantage given that there can be few more necessary cultural lessons than survival. Most of us attend to them carefully enough, even if to forget or briefly ignore what we've learnt once teenaged immortality kicks in and risk begins to feel life-affirming. Joe doesn't care for my opinion about danger even now, having no faculty for judging the magnitude of a risk (for which 'Will it kill me?' would be a start) and not even understanding the notion that there can be degrees of probability of harm. That is, he doesn't know how serious it could be, nor how likely. He's unaware of many of these ordinary practicalities of negotiating life's hazards quite simply because he's cut off from the lessons of other people's experience. It's often said of children, and in Joe's case it's often literally true: he can't be told.

The writer Francis Spufford finds children in that condition unbearable: 'locked in their innocence, tottering through a world they don't understand in the misplaced confidence that it's safe'.

Simple enough to put them right, surely? As I watch Joe tottering through the world, I think how short, how vivid, how pregnant a word is 'danger', and for all those reasons how bloody insufferably impossible to convey its meaning to him. So it is that our differences from Joe lurk among the obvious – obvious to us, that is – everyday things we take for granted, suggesting perhaps that those simple things are not so trivial, that sophisticated existence turns on small cogs, making me think how complacent I am about how remarkable people are, how it is that extraordinary things tend to happen when you can't do the ordinary, and how we should look with less complacency on our simple selves.

After nearly ten years of looking after Joe, we were running out of steam, at the point of accepting that we could no longer customise his future. Our problem was not controlling him – we managed that passably well – it was controlling the world. His mother in particular had devoted herself to creating a unique environment for Joe that required the help of a small legion of remarkable carers with an extravagant degree of commitment. They were hard to find and hard to keep, the whole operation like running a small business.

One after another, Josie, Joanna and the others would arrive for a morning or afternoon shift, weathering his tantrums, coaxing Joe to the table time after time, offering small rewards, working patiently through the words and locations of various body parts, the numbers and names of household objects, day after day until he got them; through prepositions, jigsaws, the names of animals and colours, encouraging him to copy letters and identify shapes, guiding his pen through miles of meandering drunken ink. Each had her style: Josie quiet and encouraging, Joanna taking no nonsense. Each, I think, grew fond of him, but everyone felt the stresses pulling at their mental seams.

The local authority finally offered adequate financial help, but little else, and securing even that had been a protracted saga of delay and denial in which all other options had to be seen to fail before Joe's home-therapy regime was approved. Yet we knew we'd been relatively lucky not to find ourselves bankrupt in the cause of Joe's education. Social services offered three hours of respite each week with a couple who seemed to be their foster-care SAS, saying they had no one else capable of meeting Joe's needs, for which read no one able to cope with him. It wasn't for want of trying. We watched a succession of confident, optimistic people sent by social services beat a swift retreat. Joe was growing bigger, stronger, more resourceful. It was increasingly unreasonable to ask others to come to the house to care for him, often on their own in a place ill-suited to the task. Meanwhile, his isolation fed a steadily more eccentric existence. The only child of comparable age with whom he had any sort of relationship was his sister and there was a crying need to try to broaden his social experience. Reason, exhaustion and the loneliness of the task were conspiring against the determination to keep him at home.

So much of what he had experienced was plain odd, between his looking-glass moment and arriving in the late-summer sunshine at Bristol. In those nine years of difference his experience, informed only by his own unique existence, was of no use outside its own narrow bounds and prepared him for nothing else.

As his mother talks to some of the senior staff, I take him round the grounds and buildings for an hour or more, introducing him to teachers and carers, showing them what he can read, some of the hundreds of words he can type on his voice-synthesising Lightwriter, how he knows colours and shapes, how he reacts to being taught, to other children and much else besides, all to see if we've found a humane place for him where a different path to experience is acceptable and not potentially fatal.

By the end of the visit his anxiety is getting the better of us, he's asking for the car and wants his Mummy to come out of that meeting room. It's a good place, though, with good people, and we agree for the first time as we leave that this is a school we could imagine him attending, if they'll have him. Climbing back into the car, Joe is happy again to be back among his family with the strange place left behind and the cosier kind of familiarity restored. Safe and sound, his mood somersaults into glee, the fear dissolves and he laughs and rocks in the seat. Within a month, he's gone.

# 3
# Obsession

Good idea, I thought, on seeing a sample school menu: wholesome, varied, organic, fresh meat and fish, steamed vegetables, brown rice; and good luck.

Plenty of children arriving here eat only one thing, they said, but all submit to sumptuous, nutritious variety, eventually. Admirable, I thought, heroic even. Yes, good luck.

Joe had been accepted by the school in Bristol. I roused myself from a slump at my desk to take the call, then sank my head in my hands and thanked God. We'd worried that it wouldn't accord with the local authority's idea of a suitable placement – too normal for him, they might say – which is why the alternatives so sacred me. As it was, the transition would be interesting enough, not least at mealtimes. Joe prefers pasta. More precisely, he prefers Sainsbury's spinach and ricotta tortellini. In fact, he's altogether rather particular about it: no other brand, no other variety, no sauce, no accompaniment and, in an ideal world, no other food. I've woken at six in the morning to feel its slithery plastic packaging pressed to my nose. He'd live on it, if allowed.

How what looks to me like green papier mâché wrapped in

yellow putty first crept into a gap in the armour-plated fastidi-ousness with which Joe was born, I haven't a clue; nor can I fathom how one mouthful became a compulsion. Suffice to say, he was soon hooked. In food, as in many habits of life, Joe tends towards a point of singularity, some powerful gravity bringing all purpose, all desire down to one irreducible, obdurate core. In all other respects this core is videos, in food it is Sainsbury's spinach and ricotta tortellini.

We invited him to broaden his experience; he disrespect-fully declined. We fought to widen his vision; he rebelled with the squint-eyed focus of an infant Clint Eastwood. We steered him towards other foods he tolerated such as peanut butter sandwiches, baked beans, chips or yoghurts. He veered like a somnolent driver, always back to pasta. A packet serving two adults wasn't enough, at neither the first serving nor sometimes the second. His appetite was wolfish and as so often when resisting his monomania, I felt like the lamb who might also be devoured.

One day at Sainsbury's we turned into a parking space and before I'd pulled the keys from the ignition he'd unclipped his belt and wellied open the door. It swung wide with a pop art 'clunk' – right into the navy-blue estate next to us. His timing was impeccable. The woman pushing her shopping trolley to a stop on the path by the parking bays was the driver. Through the windscreen, I watched her gasp.

The metallic thump on her bodywork hit her like concus-sion, but Joe, oblivious, shameless, just hurtled past. He didn't worry, didn't know. She couldn't believe that, caught in the act, he didn't care, and wouldn't have thought much of his sense of priorities. Little did she know there was pasta at stake. I could sense her simmering temptation to clip him round the ear. I sympathised, but wearily. One learns to shrug at Joe, each time he despatches some valued item into the void, but shrugging takes practice and the poor lady hadn't previously experienced the collateral damage of Joe's single-mindedness, wasn't yet inured to the material loss.

'Joe!' I thundered, to impress her rather than chastise him, since he barely registered the tone of voice and stopped only to wait for me. Down the side of the door of the blue car was a long, hazy red stripe. A couple of minutes with a wipe steadily erased the mark and she was generous enough to leave with only an apology. Joe had just one thing on his mind and we were off at a canter as soon as I joined him.

On occasion, after I'd summoned courage to bully him into eating something new, he'd be sick. Whether the antipathy was physical or psychological, I couldn't tell; the vomit was authentic.

'Ick,' says Joe, with comic matter-of-factness.

'Ick,' he says, as if noting a curious change in the weather, until I say it too.

'Yes, Joe. Sick. The wind shifting northerly, I see.' And I fetch a cloth.

His Lightwriter is a device like a lap-top incorporating a voice-synthesiser which supplements Joe's limited spoken vocabulary. He types the word and the machine speaks it. One day when the cupboard was bare, the spelling he was working towards turned out to be 'Sainsbury'. Any carrier bag with that name began to be ransacked, contents spread across the table, onto the floor, yoghurts splatting open while I tried to restrain him. Finding a packet, he'd cling to it from his mother's house to mine or back again; he'd take it to bed at night; he'd emerge from the kitchen waving a carving knife to have it opened and press a saucepan, colander and plate on me in rapid succession. His spoken word for pasta is 'pak'; three letters in which he somehow finds room for three syllables and a three-tone melody, rising then falling. Even obsession can sound lyrical. We heard the song of 'pak' frequently; and 'mo [more] pak' nearly as often.

Joe, like many children with autism – like many children – aches for familiarity. Endless repetition is a hallmark of his everyday life: the same songs, same games, same food, same routines. When we sing 'Old Macdonald' I supplement it with Makaton, a much-simplified version of British Sign Language, where pigs are a circling fist in front of the nose and horses clip-clop with two fingers of one hand astride the sideways palm of the other. In our version, each animal has a unique way of tickling Joe, and through the grunts and neighs and moos I think to myself, How many times is that? When we finish, Joe shouts: 'Genn!'

'Genn!'

And we sing it again.

'Genn!'

And again. As the herds of pigs and horses and cows multiplied over the years and Old Macdonald no doubt survived on the subsidies and fretted over the paperwork, I used to wonder how many hundreds there'd been. Now I wonder if I should wonder in thousands.

Pasta and videos, though, form the steady pulse of his obsession. The videos had to be known videos, the same few played eternally. New ones didn't much register unless they included familiar characters, in which case they'd be tolerated until recognised frame by frame and then also admitted to the canon of fixation. Other obsessions I could imagine fading one day, these never would. The school didn't ban them so much as ignore their existence; children of Joe's age not normally being allowed techno-toys of any kind, videos, computers, CD players and the like. No doubt about it, I thought: good luck.

He spent the first few days at school with one of us at his side until bedtime and he was reassured we'd be there in the morning, but he wasn't happy. He needed constant comforting, his face clouded with terror whenever I moved away, he resisted the involvement of others, he wanted to go home. Unsurprisingly so, since all was new: the people, the place, the food and many everyday events, as custom and habit were all but wiped clean. Of course, there were tight new routines at all points of the day, but it's hard to imagine how alien they must have first appeared, how terrible the initial shock of dislocation. One evening at about eight o'clock I looked at my watch and became aware of a sense of relief – knowing Joe was at last asleep and the day's unhappiness over. That I was more comfortable thinking him unconscious speaks as much to my guilt as to his misfortune, for there was a nagging archetype of fatherly provider in the back of my mind, insisting that I ought to make things better for him, lift his misery, and yet, though I could think of many ways in which his new life was imperfect, my ability to improve it was exhausted. The school life was the best on offer, not least because the surer route to deeper unhappiness for Joe was to give in to his limpet-like obsessions.

I found myself clinging to a paradoxical hope: that Joe's fondness for routine, if at first making the novelty of his surroundings more upsetting, would in time loosen and displace the hold of routines past. For the novel would soon become the new routine, loved as much as the old had been, and the old, once so captivating, would become merely memory. I found that I was depending for the sake of Joe's happiness on being supplanted in his life by a keener attachment to whatever was now happening every day. There's a difference, of course, between fondness for routine and love of individuals, but I think less so in Joe's case, since other people are most dear to him in great part to the extent to which they are predictable and dependable. There is a sense for Joe in which quantity will often be quality, and he will love more that which he experiences most often. At least, I half hoped so.

One of the reasons we chose the school was because it didn't show videos. We'd counted our bruises and concluded he was better behaved when denied. Most schools capitulate to the craving, which is common among autistic children, the staff finding the respite doubly irresistible: it stops the whining and the child is occupied. We knew from experience that this was a delusive peace, that it would be a short-term respite and a self-defeating one, for videos are Joe's lotus fruit: exquisitely delicious to him but poison to his wider attention. They sap every desire for any kind of existence away from the screen, and so the more he watches, the more he craves. Unchecked, he would descend into a world of videos everlasting.

'He'd climb,' says his mother, 'over my dead body for a video.' No one, I should say, loves him more, but you can pour love and energy into Joe and feel snubbed for a glimpse of Postman Pat. It's best not to take it personally.

'Bless him!' say those who've mostly not experienced his stamina. 'Children. They do pester, don't they?' Friends remark that all children like routine, all children like what they know, all are obsessive at times. Such commonplaces offer reassurance: 'Don't panic, mine do it too. Joe isn't unusual, and anyway, how bad can it be? One shouldn't fret about a little repetitive behaviour in one's children.'

I'm grateful for the intended consolation but, truly, they have no idea. For there's the obsession of normal children and there's Joe. Let me try to put it into perspective. If Joe found on escaping to various neighbours' houses that he was in a nirvana of endless videos, he might have popped home briefly to refuel with pasta, but never again to stay. Never. He knows his priorities. Think drug-crazed, fanatical, murderous desperation; think lawless smack habit; think this without exaggeration; think it seriously. There's a phrase used of Olympic champions and artists devoted to their craft: single-minded. Imagine this with absurd literality: a mind with one objective only, a single thought driving out all others, the thought of an obsessive lover, a glutton on a fast, a drowning man.

Picture him smashing his head on a lamppost when an expected glimpse of a video box, never mind the film itself, failed to materialise because the library was unexpectedly closed. Think of the time Joe and I called on a friend in St Albans. We allowed him a bare minute to explore as she and I chatted in the hall on the way out, only to hear within moments the sound of a wild thrashing of the upright piano in the next room. Was he playing it, or demolishing it? I dropped my coat and followed the noise to find him staging an assault on the piano like a cliff face, after establishing base camp on the keyboard he now searched, scrambled, stomped up and down looking for a foothold to take him higher, having already discovered by practical trial that the music stand was too fragile to take his weight, and left it dangling from a hinge.

At the summit – of both the piano and Joe's ambition – was a shelf stacked with video tapes, supposedly far enough out of reach to deter any sane child's attempt, but not out of sight and therefore not high enough to deter Joe. I reached out to lift him – higher, he assumed; lower, I intended – and barely held his weight as he leant precariously out of my arms reaching, complaining longingly to the last.

Think of him ripping through any shop, sprinting (in his fashion) to the rows of tapes, and then from shop to shop and back again, cracking open empty box after empty box. Imagine him trashing any home, turning out cupboards faster than I can stuff the contents back, scouring under tables, standing in the centre of a room and scrutinising every surface, every nook, every plausible hiding place, gauging its potential.

Or think, perhaps most bizarrely of all, of the day we bought a cooker hood. Scan those words if you will for a clue as to why a cooker hood would incite Joe's frenzy. It sat, this innocuous thing, fresh in its box with the manufacturer's name and the words 'cooker hood' printed on each side. Joe saw it, his mouth dropped open, his expression intensified, he gazed hard at the box. Then he set about it, snatching at the corners, trying feverishly to find a way past packaging, tape and staples. Curious, I thought, that Joe should show much interest in a sealed box. There was a time when we could leave his Christmas present in an open paper bag on the kitchen table and he wouldn't be tempted to peek. I assume that all he saw was a paper bag, unable to conceive that it had contents. But this box, what was it about this box?

I began cutting through the tape, trying to calm him, hoping he'd relax once the thing inside proved unfamiliar and uninteresting. Joe pulled at loose pieces of cardboard, flinging out polystyrene packaging, driven by a disturbing sense of purpose, until it stood, revealed: a polished, aluminium cooker hood.

'See, Joe, it's a cooker hood. Nothing in it for you, I'm afraid.'

Joe wasn't satisfied. He went back to the discarded box to touch the words on its side, and at last it dawned on me: 'Hood'. In Joe's mind the word had an inseparable prefix: 'Robin'. Not because of any fascination for historical myth, but because

Walt Disney produced the video with a sly fox playing the lead. I should have realised, 'Hood' being the shorthand he'd sometimes type into his Lightwriter if, for whatever reason, this film was where his obsession had come to rest that day.

'No, Joe, it's not Hood, not Robin Hood. It's for the cooker. For cooking, Joe.'

Cooking is a word he half understands as a precursor to serving him pasta and involving – for what purpose he fails to appreciate – the gas hob. That is, he understands 'cooking' as part of a process, a sequence like A ... B ... C ..., rather than having any particular utility. He fails to see that the essence of 'cooking' is that things should have time to cook, that 'cooking' actually cooks the food, and so he would turn off the hob the instant it had been turned on, if I didn't stop him. Done that bit, now serve. So the word 'cooking' would make little sense in this context, having what meaning it does only in the other, pasta-specific one. He finds it extraordinarily hard to move thoughts between the two: 'Cooking cannot possibly mean anything in relation to this big silver contraption, because cooking means what happens before I'm fed pasta.' With time and more experience, 'cooking' also came to mean to Joe the routine that delivered his beans or chips. But for Joe, these ideas are reluctant to leave their particulars for the world of abstraction, and so the words are slow to acquire a general sense which can be used in diverse contexts. A recent account of autism describes a child who learnt laboriously to spread butter on bread and finally mastered the movement, but was helpless again when faced with jam. Because explanation, like definition, often requires such a mental transfer of ideas from one context to another, much goes misunderstood by Joe.

A box, on the other hand, that has the word 'Hood' on the side, must strike him as akin to many other boxes with 'Hood' on the side. Such boxes in his experience have always meant only one thing. A useless effort at explanation, then, my attempt to locate this hood in the world of cooking: not much sense for Joe to take from that. How ludicrous that the distinction proves so tricky, though admittedly not one I'm accustomed to making, between the hood that hid our hero's head from the Sheriff's men and the hood that inhales kitchen odours.

I knew with sinking heart that the struggle for enlightenment was already lost. No surprise then that he still wasn't satisfied and now demanded that the cooker hood be turned upside down. That was easy. The next was not.

'Oop,' he said.

'Open? I can't open it, Joe, it's a cooker hood. *Cooker* hood, not *Robin* Hood; cooker, not a video, Joe.'

But I could open it, and we did, taking out the clear plastic panels to show him the light bulbs lying within, removing the grille to explore the ventilation channels inside, peering down the hole where the chimney flu was to fit.

He was determined to pull it apart, no matter that the most limited spatial awareness would have told him there was no room for a video in the few cubic millimetres of confined darkness so far unexplored. Yet his hopefulness endured. It wasn't until I'd fixed the blasted thing in position – I cursed it now for being careless of its name – wired it up and turned it on nearly an hour later that he began to lose faith … and exploded into a short-lived tantrum of heaving sobs and blows to his head, thwarted and miserable, hitherto devout in the belief that this pyramid-like lump of metal, with every crevice investigated, must hide some secret chamber where he'd find the intoxicating moving images promised by those four letters. For some weeks afterwards he'd call me into the kitchen and gesture towards it with a quizzical look.

When Joe seizes every possibility of a video and holds fast until all hope is dead, and when false hope proves so hard to kill, surviving on misunderstandings that would take him a whole lifetime's education to correct, when neither reason nor evidence can persuade, when so much conspires against calm, his obsession might endure on a bad day from the first minute of waking until his eyes close with the last. Perhaps that gives some measure of his single-mindedness. If you continue to doubt, note, finally, that Joe can spot the spine of *Wallace and Gromit's Grand Day Out*, or any other favourite, at a hundred paces, then look into his crazed eyes as he scrambles out of his seat belt, heart pounding, whenever we even park on another driveway, and tell me all children are like that.

And yet, Joe's obsession is one of the most glaring but intellectually elusive quirks of his behaviour. The lessons from it are hard to draw since, to some extent, my friends are right when they say that many children want high degrees of familiarity and routine, and all can become fixated on the toy they can't live without, the now dog-eared book they still prefer to all others, the blanket they must clasp to their cheek before they can sleep, on trains or tractors, on a jumper or on pink.

The difference between this and the autistic child is one mainly of degree, but what a degree. At Joe's first special-needs school, a local authority day school in south Watford for children with moderate learning difficulties, one boy would insist when shopping with his mother that she bought identical goods in exactly the same sequence every time. If she failed to keep to the routine – at any point – then, no, it was all wrong, it didn't make sense – Mummy buys two pints of full-cream milk then strawberry yoghurt from the middle shelf, that's Mummy, and we didn't do that and so if that's wrong then you're wrong, and I'm in the wrong place, and you're not really my mummy and I want my mummy and … whaaaaaa!

His sense of security depended on a routine of rigid consistency. Here, in a supermarket he'd visited countless times, he found his life unravelling, found normal coordinates unreliable because one scuff of detail was wrong, became terrified, suspicious of a world in which lack of consistency meant lost identity. The school tried to teach him to tolerate change by using small picture cards to represent all his normal activities, placing them in the expected order and familiarising him with the correspondence between the picture strip and his daily routine. One day, with tenderness and patience, the staff began to show him that two cards could swap places, and then perhaps be returned to their original position. On another day, the cards might swap places and stay there for a while. But look, both were still there, swimming hadn't gone, it was still on his activity strip, just relocated, and so the world was changing identity, merely rearranging, slightly, its appearance. Once comfortable with the idea that the cards could move, the same variation was introduced to his routine, I believe with success.

This difference of degree between, if I may call it, normal and abnormal obsession, is so wide as to hint at a more fundamental deficit. It's clear that these children find comfort, reassurance, security in their obsessions, as well as hypnotic fascination. Why should they need such extreme repetition, why return so magnetically again and again to the same movements, the same images, reluctant to move on? What is it about the way they see the world, compared with the way we see it, that makes it so slippery, so dangerously inconsistent?

I think the first part of the answer is that, whereas most of us have little difficulty recognising continuity amid change, autistic children find their sense of the stability of things easily threatened. At the extremes, this sets their world spinning, but even in lesser cases the mental adjustment, the reclassification of things and their attributes, requires, I suspect, far more conscious reorientation for them than for us. We know Mummy is still Mummy through any number of innovations in shopping habit and we know it without hesitation. The problem for some of those with autism is that even small changes seem capable of jolting their sense of continuity to the point of vertiginous insecurity and it takes time to get back on a firm footing. Joe is not remotely so severe a case as his former schoolmate, but it's clear that change holds little attraction for him. What, for

of the fact that when taking him
...reful to avoid wetting my hair? Not
...vould soon agree, but because it makes
...tnessing my mop turned sleek and drip-
...comes uncertain bordering terrified. If I
appro... ...vay. The sound of my voice seems to help,
but as I speak ... assure him, though he might be coaxed to
come nearer, he raises a hand as if to protect himself and tentatively reaches out to prod my hair, a sour grimace wrinkling
his nose and curling his lip, before flinching away again and
turning to play elsewhere.

The child who put all his trust in me a few moments ago
when I flung him, screeching, ecstatic, through the water by
arms or legs, or held him, arm-bands cast aside, in the deep
end of the pool, now reacted to my wet hair as if … as if
what? Threatening, disgusting maybe? Neither, I think, given
his consistent indifference to the wet heads swimming, playing, bobbing and diving all around him. So why did I unnerve
him when others didn't? Perhaps because they were strangers
anyway. Could it be that the detail of wet hair turned me into
a stranger too? Had I become unreliable, discontinuous with
the daddy he thought he knew?

A quick experiment one day would show if I could conquer
Joe's apparent perception of discontinuity, if that's what it was:
I stood in front of him, dry-headed, and then ducked down for
a second, coming up wet in the same spot, obvious to anyone
else that I was the same person if only because space and time
conspired against any impostor. To Joe, that logical impossibil-

ity made no difference; still I could see the forehead frown, the eyes widen, the mouth sneer; still he doubted and shrank. Joe, it seemed, wasn't entirely sure if I was still Daddy, or, if I was, whether my Daddy-ness was now dangerously compromised, and not until we'd begun to dry ourselves and my hair turned less slick, more recognisably dishevelled, did he regain full confidence in me.

In an arresting passage in his novel *The Corrections*, Jonathan Franzen describes the shifting, deceptive sensory world of the mind of Alfred, a sufferer of Parkinson's disease:

> In the manner of a wheat seedling thrusting itself up out of the earth, the world moved forward in time by adding cell after cell to its leading edge, piling moment on moment, and that to grasp the world even in its freshest, youngest moment provided no guarantee that you'd be able to grasp it again a moment later ... no sooner had he reconfirmed [the present] than the leading edge of time added yet another layer of new cells, so that he again faced a new and ungrasped world; which was why, rather than exhaust himself playing catch-up, he preferred more and more to spend his days down among the unchanging historical roots of things.

Could such a sense of the confounded slipperiness of things through time be one of the spurs to a love of routine, even to obsessive repetition; an attempt to grasp and hold still the otherwise giddying shiftiness and unreliability of things, to hold tight to what's known and liked? I'm not sure. There are probably other things going on, but I suspect that something of this sort, to some degree, is at play in Joe and others like him.

Most of us are plainly not so troubled. One capacity making us more comfortable sliding around amid change and impermanence, happier to cope with the torrent of flux, is our instinctive essentialism. Whereas Joe and other autistic children often insist on the same, we make do with, even welcome, the same sort. In the case of people we know, we believe that their essence continues independently of changes in their appearance or behaviour, whether as a result of ageing, wetting their hair, changing their shopping habits, or even losing limbs; we know that people's bodies can appear differently but their essence remains. This knowledge applied to innumerable everyday experiences lessens the shock of the new by helping us identify elements of familiarity. Essence is problematical for autistic children because it is an abstraction, an idea, and Joe is a boy who lives in a world of physical particulars.

Our essentialism is no small achievement. One corollary, for example, is that we are fantastically skilled at categorisation, recognising shared characteristics, believing that certain objects have a nature in common even though they look different. Psychologists now believe normal children at nine months understand that objects of the same category share hidden properties. By two years old they demonstrate an understanding of the difference between an internal core and external appearance. The American psychologist Paul Bloom says that young children have a sense that what matters is on the inside, and describes an experiment in which

> children were shown pictures of a series of transformations where animals were gradually modified in their appearance: a porcupine was surgically altered to resemble a cactus; a tiger was stuffed into a lion suit so that it looked like a lion; a real dog was modified to look like a toy. When the transformations were radical enough, the children … insisted that it was still a porcupine, a tiger, and a dog, regardless of what it looked like. In a child's mind, to be a specific animal is to have more than just a certain appearance, it is to have a certain internal structure. It is only when the transformations are described as changing the innards of the animals – presumably, their essences – that children, like adults, take them as changing the type of animal itself.

Essentialism has a long philosophical pedigree, from Aristotle's notion of quiddity, or 'whatness', to John Locke's *Essay Concerning Human Understanding*. In Book III of the *Essay* he writes:

> Essence may be taken for the very being of anything, whereby it is what it is. And thus the real internal, but generally (in substances) unknown constitution of things, whereon their discoverable qualities depend, may be called their essence. This is the proper original signification of the word, as is evident from the formation of

it; essentia, in its primary notation, signifying properly, being. And in this sense it is still used, when we speak of the essence of particular things, without giving them any name.

'The very being of anything' ought to be able to cope with a bad hair day. Yet in some autistic children, though not quite in Joe, the normal ability to categorise according to some deep essence is apparently so deficient that they seem to take to heart a famous paradox coined by Kung-sun Lung in the third century to the effect that 'a white horse is not a horse', meaning that any single, particular horse by its very particularity ceases to be of the general category of horses – horses in abstract – which can have no particular colour. The rest of us are able to hold in mind the particular and its essence at the same time: the fluffy pink cow, the plastic cow, the picture of a cow, the vast lumbering pat-splattered real cow are all, we know, at some level the same thing.

Perhaps repetition is Joe's attempt to hold on to precisely one particular as a substitute for the familiarity the rest of us find in essence. Paul Bloom, writing of the normal way in which we order our perceptions, says: 'Our minds have evolved to put things into categories and to ignore or downplay what makes these things distinct ... what all categories share is that they capture a potential infinity of individuals under a single perspective. They lump.' That is, ignoring differences can be as important as observing them. Maybe autistic children simply find it harder to put distinguishing details aside, paying too much heed to difference and failing to appreciate sufficiently those elements of similarity. To use Paul Bloom's distinction, borrowed from Darwin, they split when they should lump. Why does the brain usually choose the latter, he asks. His answer is derived from Locke: 'Without categories, everything is perfectly different from everything else, and nothing can be generalized and learned … Without concepts, we are helpless.'

The conceptual is a dry form of education. We much prefer to take our lessons from the personal, the particular, but Bloom is surely right that without the conceptual we become lost amid innumerable, unconnected particulars with no relevance beyond themselves. Though we might find it uncongenial, we also depend on the conceptual for much of our understanding of the everyday world that would otherwise seem, as I suspect it seems to Joe and those like him, capable of terrifying volatility. The vivid and the particular engage our passions, but if we are not to be swarmed by them, we must classify.

Joe finds some categories easier than others. When he was seven or eight we spent many hours asking him to place pictures of related objects into the same pile – clothes, food, vehicles. Progress was extraordinarily slow. He had immense difficulty understanding that some quality linked shoes and T-shirts, for example, or cars and trains. The category of 'things to eat' was easier, even if, as was usually the case, he didn't eat them personally. Nevertheless, socks would sometimes finish up in the food pile. Dogs, though varying in size from rat to brown bear, are also somehow recognisably the same thing to him. He had no trouble working out that cars all have the potential to take him somewhere he wants to go, regardless of make, colour or model. He uses the word 'book' for anything that's held in the hand and read – magazine, newspaper, book, leaflet, letter. 'Wet' applies to just about any liquid in any form. Coaxing him to taste sweets he'd not tasted before, even to play with a new toy, could be a labour of many months, and this seemed partly because he doubted their essential similarity to others of the same kind, didn't perhaps see them as being of a kind that mattered to him. A corresponding difficulty is that when he does recognise something as of an ilk, he expects it to behave exactly as others he has known, so that any computer he sits at will surely, he thinks, be loaded with his favourite games. And any box with 'Hood' on it …

One or two of these categories – toys and sweets – are brightly wrapped or brightly plastic enough to promise a familiar pleasure, and most children readily succumb. Joe is seldom tempted. Other intransigencies, such as his unwillingness to try new food or new activities, are familiar to many parents, though some will be overcome by childish curiosity. In Joe's case, no such counterbalancing imperative serves to extend his experience; if he is to venture more widely, he has to be led, kicking and screaming if need be.

This is another exception to the obsession of those with autism and the obsession of the rest of us: theirs is more stubborn. Joe's persistence is something else.

'Noo,' says Joe, his word for video (origin a mystery).

'No, Joe, no noo at Daddy's house today.'

'Noo!'

'No, Joe, no noo today.'

'Noo!' the long vowel straining plaintively in his throat.

So he drags a chair from the kitchen with the idea of clambering to the top of the bookshelves to some spot where he'd once, perhaps three years past, seen a video in hiding. He was once found swinging from the top of a kitchen cupboard door, screaming and frantic as his grip began to fail, left dangling when the chair beneath him tipped over during an illicit scout for videos.

'Oh, but he enjoys them so much, surely he can have one now and then?' Almost anyone who's heard of Joe will say as much. What harm would it do? What cruelty to deny to a child who endures such frustration in life this one greatest pleasure? The unforgiving fact is that Joe is calmer, happier, when consistently told 'no'. To offer hope that I'll give way occasionally is to feed an insatiable agitation. There's some sickness, surely, some monstrous sadism in life's joke that leaves him most disturbed by what he most enjoys, then makes temptation ubiquitous.

We've struggled with the problem for years, trying intermittently to use videos as motivators, promised in return for some good work or behaviour ('He loves them so. Surely we can get him to do something constructive to earn one?'). But he was motivated only to skimp the work, the more quickly to demand the reward. On other occasions we tried to ration them rigidly on the grounds that the world was full of the pernicious things and creating a video-free environment for Joe was unrealistic. Thus the attempt to create discipline, not denial.

Whatever we tried, we failed, as the hours spent watching were either steadily ratcheted up to appease his distress, or became hours of imminent torture as with tears and ferocious tantrums Joe raged against the limitations set on his viewing. The more he had, the more he wanted. Zero tolerance is not an idea I care for, but it's all we have. During those optimistic, misguided episodes when we thought we could control his obsession, Joe would start by being allowed one video a week, or perhaps one at his mother's house and one at mine. He adapted to this routine by clamouring for a video the second he walked through the door; as the final credits rolled, he was clamouring to go back again. To hear a child pining for his mother tugs at your heart, and some of it was genuine, but the rest was fraud: he was pining mostly for Postman Pat.

'Mee,' he says (from the second syllable of Mummy).

'Mee, mee!' over and over again.

Joe's accidentally cruel genius was to compound my feelings of inadequacy at failing to calm his obsession by also spurning me now I'd served my purpose. In war, we applaud ruthlessness like that; perhaps that's why caring for Joe had the ring of shellfire. I knew his incessant 'Mee' was partly a means to an end, just as 'Dee' might become his passion once his mother had exhausted her usefulness in turn, and so I had to suspend my nature, stop thinking as a father, to appreciate that this was rejection with no hurt imagined or intended; he simply had other things on his mind.

Another failure was our belief that we could limit the hypnotic effect of videos by preventing Joe from rewinding and replaying the same scene – when Postman Pat falls down the hill in the snow, when the tree blows over in *Winnie the Pooh* – replaying it perhaps twenty times before moving on. It made no difference, he was hooked on any terms, and in this state of relentless, nagging disquiet he'd pester and pester and pester; he'd type on his Lightwriter over and over again different formulations of the same desire and then hit the speak button repeatedly:

'good boy joe video yes', its mechanical staccato voice would say before I interrupted and typed once more the answer he'd already heard innumerable times that day:

'sleep first then mummy'

That is, he must wait until the following day. He would erase it and write instead:

'no sleep car red video pat'

Or

'pasta first then video'

'i want video'

'video yes mummy soon'

You have to admire his versatility, his relentless ingenuity, his incorrigible disregard for the slow shredding of my placidity. I can't ignore him, believe me I've tried. He's liable to take silence as denial, not just for the present but for all time. His appeals become more agonised and frantic, he hits his head and face with hands and fists, shouting 'noo' and throwing either himself onto the chair or objects around the room, down the stairs, at me or Cait. 'Sleep first' was my pitiful compromise between offering consolation ('yes, you will have another before long') and restraining his appetite ('but not yet').

And on they would go, these interminable mechanical requests, until I'd take away his Lightwriter and put it out of reach, take away the machine we bought to give him a voice, a voice which that day I could no longer stand. At such moments, he cared for nothing in the world apart from videos and snarled at whatever I dared suggest by way of distraction. In this battle of wills my own was a paltry thing, hopelessly outgunned. I hung on only because the distant alternative was far, far worse.

So it was that on reflection after a day in the trenches we plucked up courage to ban videos, threw them out, and faced two or three unrelenting weeks of the drug abuser's cold turkey with not even those hours in front of the screen to relieve Joe's mania. When we took that nuclear option, we broke his heart, and felt his despair would break ours. But with time, most sadness mends, vicious cycles can break, and two or three weeks was about the norm (we went through it more than once) before he began slowly to calm down and become the happier, more-rounded child we knew he could be, his demonic possession never quite exorcised but at least at bay.

Were we right? I don't know. Would it be more humane to allow Joe to have his fill, sit in front of limitless videos, let him enjoy this rare, exultant thrill – to give in? Tomorrow would be easier, that's for sure, but would he then be lost to reality, hypnotically sealed in a flickering landscape inhabited by Disney, Postman Pat, Fireman Sam and the Teletubbies? We aspire to as much normality in Joe's life as his disability permits, but sometimes, when I wonder whether normality provides much nourishment to Joe, the video netherworld seems not so unreasonable. I don't know the right course even now, and simply offer this: the more he watches, the more aggressive he becomes, the less tolerant, the more obsessive about all things, the less interested in the world outside, the more remote from other people and the less civilised (or do I mean human?).

In a recent report, his schoolteacher wrote: 'Left to his own devices his repertoire of activities will quickly become limited and predictable.' It would, I suspect, become monotonous in the extreme. The word video is now taboo, except once a year at Christmas when Joe is permitted to watch one – a strange conception of Christmas but as good as any he's likely to understand. If the taboo word is spoken within his hearing we all skip a beat for fear of his reaction and have acquired the habit of using words like 'tape' or 'vid' or spelling it out instead. Our perverse hope, given that we yearn for Joe to learn, is that this code will be secure from the catastrophe of him understanding. Nowadays the closest he comes to watching a video – Christmas excepted – is to stare at the thumbnail adverts for them in children's magazines, or once in a while to stand in a shop, open empty boxes and linger over pictures of Peter Pan or the Aristocats. Ah, he loves them so, I think to myself, seeing the yearning in his face. Surely just one wouldn't hurt? We've all felt the pull, all been beguiled by Joe's forlorn desperation, all betrayed our better judgement, all regretted it.

It's not unusual for autistic children to seem possessed. I've read of an obsession for sugar so consuming that one boy, given the chance, would sit with a spoon and eat to the bottom of a two-pound bag of Tate and Lyle; of a fascination with emptying the contents of cereal packets, or pouring liquids down the drain: shampoo, washing-up liquid, fresh milk. Washing machines are often a favourite; vacuum cleaners another. It seems likely that some of the appeal is hypnotic – a sense of poetry in sinuous, fluid movement or beauty in mechanical cause and effect, some music in the cascade of cornflakes to the floor, some dance in the coloured jumble in the washing machine – and the children do have a trance-like air about them. Sometimes they will seem to conjure physical excitement from nowhere, flapping their hands or shaking their heads. One word used to describe this is 'stimming' – self-stimulating behaviour – a kind of feedback, a loop between causing an action and becoming caught up within it. With his whole body, Joe will rhythmically buck himself off the bed with massive energy, like yogic flying, laughing hysterically, as each bounce propels him into the next movement, again and again, a flapping fish on the dockside. Watching a video, he surges forward and back as if urging the action on, and is further mesmerised as the scene unfolds.

I'm aware of eliding a number of characteristics here, but it strikes me that there's continuity between routine, leading to repetition and obsession on the one hand, and the difficulty in making sense of novelty on the other, observed perhaps in the fact that some children with autism will withdraw to the inner consolation of stimming when most troubled by unfamiliar external events. They have the appearance of fending off what they don't know by hanging on to the skirts of what they do, normal enough among all children, but here carried to an obsessive excess.

Even though life is now video-free, at least as free as it can be given high-street window displays, Joe's obsessive nature is still not entirely contained, but seeps into every occasion. Once in a while we zip along the A41 to my parents' house in Hertfordshire, nestling half an hour away in the Chiltern Hills. Over time, Joe has learnt the refrain he now performs from the moment the car is parked there to the moment we leave.

The car door opens, he canters up the drive, rings the door-bell, steps back three paces. The front door swings wide, he hurtles inside, dashes into the living room and stands a few feet short of the television to pick out any videos he recognises. They've all been removed. He comes out of the living room, goes into the kitchen, opens the fridge, asks for microwave chips – no pasta here, he knows – sits under the stairs to eat them, asks for another packet, settles for a sandwich, eats it, jumps up, asks for juice, drinks half, pours the rest down the sink. Back into the living room he pulls at the sliding patio door until we open it, goes outside and asks me to throw a large sponge ball high into the air which he fetches a dozen times and lobs back to me before finally flinging it into the vegetable patch. Then I throw it onto the roof and we watch it tumble down. He gets bored and runs round the outside of the house to the front door, rings the bell again, laughs when someone opens the door, comes in, charges through the hall, into the living room and leaves again by the patio door, five times, or thereabouts. Then he opens the back door to the annex, plays at slamming it until I fear for the glass and throw a towel over the top to soften the impact. He goes upstairs to sit in Grandma's bed, sings to himself, comes down, asks me to join him. We play in the bed, he sits in the other beds, he asks to go home, asks many times, and eventually we do. The order might vary slightly. I do mean slightly. Lately, the whole performance has tended to accelerate. As if on speed, he now blasts along on a breathless charge from one scene to the next. Move over the Reduced Shakespeare Company. Joe knows the plot backwards but usually plays it only one way.

This is the child we took from a life defined intensely by sameness and put in a place where all was strange, a sheep at sea, a chimp in the Arctic, little that was recognisable. To Joe too, in my thoughts, I whispered 'good luck'.

So worried was I about his proclivity for adopting stock behaviours, like the lazy owner of a thin phrase book, that I also thought there was potential for any trouble in his first days at school to be quickly cemented into habit. Instead of growing accustomed to his new surroundings and new routines, instead of settling in, I asked, would he settle into a pattern of riot? If so, time, the healer, would not help but rather consolidate all that was going wrong as, through repetition, new tools of rebellion found permanence in his arsenal.

In short, the school's intimidating initial task was to try to restrain Joe's high-pressure tendency to become a runaway train. We thought he had been well behaved immediately before he started, but we had the advantage of knowing his idiosyncrasies, knowing which techniques worked to apply the brakes, and we had only one strange child to worry about. There's no disguising the brutality of his removal, not far short of kidnap I should think, and all concerned were steeled for the weeks ahead as we found out whether he would adapt. There's uncertainty about the prospects of all children, though perhaps a little more about Joe's than most. He was on probation, no certainty he could stay if he proved unmanageable to his young carers. By Christmas, he might be out, leaving lurking in the background the familiar, almighty, stupefying question: 'Then what?' And so we began.

# 4
# Language

For days at his new school, Joe ate little. This was unnerving in a boy whose table manners were capable of striking fear into the food on his plate, but who now survived on toast at breakfast, a piece of fruit during the day and a snack in the evening, when this necessary but stringent regime relented for survival's sake. Otherwise he sat at table shoving away his plate with more or less disgust, or fled the dining room to trash his bedroom. The school's efforts were not hopeless: one day he licked a rice crispy, then thought better of it.

By the fourth week, Joe was probably beginning to realise that this was no temporary exile. One weekend Mummy would come, the next weekend Daddy. They'd see him for two days, then go again. He would stay, and the bad new ways, the unfamiliar leading edge of change, would continue to tear at the roots of everything he knew. Whatever hopes he had of being restored to comfortable old surroundings must have been steadily, pitilessly extinguished.

He was perfectly able to count the number of sleeps between one visit and the next and clung to a piece of paper on which they were ticked off. Since this became a refuge from acceptance, it was decided that the school needed a better chance to catch his attention, to stop him treating each minute of the day as time in the waiting room. We kicked away that harmful crutch and the next weekend no one came to see him – all in the cause of kindness, so we said. The following Friday he began coming home for alternate weekends.

A few weeks into this new routine Joe began banging his head on the wall at school. The first time he arrived home with a large, colourful lump above his eye, the explanations were vague and the more disconcerting for that. There was no suggestion – and no probability – that anyone did it but Joe himself, minor self-harm having been part of his volcanic repertoire for years. Taking a walk at home on one occasion soon afterwards he resisted by clouting his head several times on a brick wall, an adult hand softening the worst of the impact. What happened at school was plausibly a refinement of his technique, perhaps following the example of other children, but there was uncertainty about exactly when and why Joe did it.

Strange to think that he could plunge in an instant from apparent quietude to a shrill, despairing hell without anyone noticing why. Though sometimes unpredictable, he's not entirely irrational. The simple explanation is that there's often no way of knowing what motivates him, especially if you're not used to reading the signs, a task made harder by his steady undercurrent of emotional convulsion. His expectations and intentions can be mysterious at the best of times and the staff were quite likely unaware that Joe had been on a collision course for several minutes. For how would he tell them? Joe's language is limited and unconventional. It's easy to imagine the confusion of strangers, accustomed though they were to the weird ways of autism, trying to engage with Joe but being easily misled.

'Mee!' says Joe.

'Yes, that's right, Joe,' says his carer, thinking not unreasonably that 'Mee' means 'me'. 'You're coming too.'

Reasonable, but unhappily wrong, for Joe's 'Mee' is Mummy. It might have been a request, a yearning, and now he's been given unwitting encouragement to think his yearning might be soon satisfied.

'Mee,' says Joe again, as he hears and understands only the confirmatory 'yes' and nothing else. He's euphoric now.

'Yes, Joe, you,' says the carer, encouraged by Joe's excitement. 'We're going in the play room. And you're coming in too.' How close farce is to agony: 'Mee!' He shouts, convinced she's waiting for him behind that door, opening it, charging through in pure joy and finding, from blameless motives, an empty room. The quickest way to appease Joe is to say 'yes', but it helps to be sure what one is saying 'yes' to. And yet certainty is deceptive: there've been moments when we all thought we knew.

Or perhaps Joe's outburst was simply resistance to something he didn't like – a common reason for hitting himself in the past. Perhaps he felt his objections were ignored. They might have been; it's often right to ignore Joe's objections, even though to do so might make them more explosive.

But then, Joe often objects, often says 'no', it's one of the few words he can articulate clearly and life affords plenty of opportunity, for finding out what he wants means putting a great many choices to him.

'Do you want chips, Joe?'

'No.'

'A sandwich?'

'No.'

'Toast?'

'No.'

'Baked beans?'

'No.'

'Yoghurt?'

'No.'

'Yes' can be a while coming. On a good day, Joe's 'no' is merely put-upon, a mildly truculent 'no', a 'no' that seems to say 'what are you bothering me with that for?' or 'don't be ridiculous'.

On a bad day, his 'no' rattles defiance, a spitting little Alamo to your theoretically mightier but fainter-hearted 'yes'. On a very bad day, 'no' becomes a growl, a javelin thrower's Neanderthal grunt. The sound he makes begins like the nasal whine of a distant small aircraft closing swiftly and climaxes with a bark of menacing, teeth-baring ferocity.

'NnnnAGH!'

When wielded with real intent, he somehow blends in a screech. The overall effect, I say it with pride, is awesome: ferocity mingled with fear, hostility with deep grievance as we move with instant escalation from my harmless question to his rabid stand-off. Of course I wish he didn't but, since he does, I can't help admiring the conviction.

Language is said to be a human instinct. To see something of the basis of this instinct, the skills on which it depends, and how falteringly for Joe, we need think only of the character of his 'no', think of his response to the most elementary yes-or-no questions. Only then do we appreciate that the linguistic distance between Joe and everyone else is not due only to his limited vocabulary, only then do we see the bear traps in every encounter.

His pantomimic over-reactions suggest he misjudges questions offering a direct choice of the most basic kind, however simply phrased. 'Would you like X?' is a neutral inquiry, it has no emotional emphasis – though it might arise from concern or compassion – and the answer doesn't particularly matter; we want merely to establish Joe's preference. Joe doesn't trust that modest ambition. Not to him well-intentioned or open-ended, questions must often be a declaration of evil intent, the start of immediate hostilities, no pause for diplomacy. He meets such confrontations, as he must judge them, with the sharpest rebuff. When he gets the wrong end of this stick the misunderstanding needs correcting fast, lest on a false premise he start beating himself up, or worse, someone else.

'OK, Joe, OK, no baked beans.'

'Baked beans gone. Look gone. Baked beans not a threat. Only asking. Gone, Joe. Away, yes. Baked beans away!'

That dealt with – you can see how cravenly – he subsides

in a blink. Sometimes it's easy for me to surrender like this; at others, when Joe's preference for doing nothing is not an option, I hold my breath for his reaction. Strongly inclined not to put on any clothes before we go out, to sit in the car for hours on end after we arrive at our destination, to say no to every turn as we drive in search of whatever it was he was agitating to get in the car for, his choices can at times be impossible. A yes of some kind is non-negotiable. If I'm unusually lucky, the confrontation will be over quickly with a sigh, and he'll bow to my insistence, but always with the kind of look that tells me he's keeping his powder dry. 'I could make your life hell, for that', his eyes suggest, 'but frankly, can't be bothered.' Otherwise, if his switch is tripped, if he can be bothered, if he determines to stand his ground, it's a determination you'll regret and every ounce of the ferocious promise of his 'no' will be royally delivered in a fierce physical rebellion of knuckles to his own face, of things thrown and broken, of endless piercing shouts and distraught lunges to the floor or into chairs, while I decide whether to wrestle him to stillness or ignore him and let the tantrum burn out.

Talking to Joe has always taken sudden, combustible turns we've quite failed to anticipate. One stray word is all it takes to light his fuse. Being so constantly on edge, wondering if lightning will strike, is emotionally exhausting, a perpetual state of resigned anxiety: it's going to happen, you know that, know you'll have to face it and maybe face it down, but you don't know when, and so must stand prepared to summon your spirit at a moment's notice for a trial of strength with a merciless bully. For sheer apprehension, life with Joe when he was at home sometimes felt as I imagine a midnight stroll through an inner-city no-go area, wondering when the blade will flash in the moonlight.

Those of us who know him fancy we've learnt to minimise, though not eliminate, accidental confrontations with Joe, but when other adults unfamiliar with what's at stake find themselves talking to him alone, the result is unpredictable.

Not far from our village there's a swimming pool, never too busy, a little stark, cold and functional, but perfectly full of water. Better still, it has wonderfully understanding staff … and a slide. A slide! You can't know what magic there used to be in that word, what manic excitability it conjured in Joe.

'Weeee,' he'd say. 'Weeee!'

'Yes, Joe. Slide.'

'Weeee,' pulling my head round to see the words formed. 'Look me in the eye, let me see your lips move and tell me it's true,' he seemed to ask.

'Yes, Joe! Swimming. Slide.'

In his most eager years, aged six or seven, we'd often go on a Saturday morning. 'Ets,' says Joe, over and over again. We think the word began as an attempt at 'wet'. Before long 'ets' began to turn up for swimming as an activity, any large body of water, rain, the bath.

Joe pulled the bag from the kitchen cupboard and made for the front door, barking 'ets!' and 'weee!' while I gathered towels and costumes. And if I didn't answer promptly: 'Dee!' 'Deee!'

'Dee!'

'Yes, Joe?'

'Ets!'

'Yes, Joe.'

Answers have a short shelf-life for Joe. It's as if they vanish from thought as soon as fade from the air, lasting no longer than the sound in his ears before the anxious desire swells again, often seconds later, and with the returning thought comes a new need for reassurance that it will truly, very shortly, be his.

'Weee!'

'Yes, Joe.'

Twenty minutes' reassurance later, we had changed and shivered up draughty stairs to the poolside. The slide was already open, a fifty-foot meander of orange and pale-blue high-sided plastic with water flowing from the top, pitching through bends down to an eighteen-inch drop into the pool below.

Children, and now and then an adult, trotted wet foot up the stairs, sat, slid, whooped, splashed, swam out and did it again, and again. A parental 'Don't run!' anxiously bossy; the children in insistent rhythm: trot, climb, slide, splash. Trot ('Don't run!'), climb, slide, splash.

Joe watched for a moment, tempted, excited, flapping as each child lurched off the end, and then pattered along to join in with arms waving gently. I took my position in the pool a few feet beyond the end of the slide to catch him on impact, before he had time to be panicked by the rush of water over his head. For the first half-dozen goes he was part of the herd: trot, climb, slide, splash, watching others in the queue, taking his turn, his excitement delicious and intoxicating.

'Genn!' he shouts, within seconds of splash-down.

'Genn!'

'OK, Joe. Again.' And I shove him up onto the poolside.

And again. Euphorically, transcendentally again, high on a rush of sensation. I love his exuberant happiness; nobody can match Joe for giddy excitement; no one has this much sheer gusto.

'Genn!'

Trot, climb, up to the top, hands on the rails, sit. It could go on for an age. But this time, abruptly, he stops. He bum-shuffles slightly to one side. He looks down along the slide, contemplates, and doesn't move. Head tilted, he gazes vaguely into space and begins chirping to himself. Behind him the queue of children becomes a sudden concertina of impatience.

The others stop at the top step to register the absent-minded boy sitting legs outstretched just to the side of pole position. Charming in hesitation, they glance about for guidance, unsure whether going down before the boy in front still constitutes a misdemeanour if he doesn't seem inclined to go down at all. Manners: so head spinning, so inconvenient when haste is the game. Between guilt and impatience they dither: 'Can we? Are we allowed to … ?' True, he didn't seem bothered, but what was he doing there? And then they go anyway, doubt overcome by energy, squeezing past, putting aside etiquette. Once one child has taken the lead with impunity the rest follow with little more than a glance. And still Joe sits.

Reactions to Joe are unpredictable, but most commonly of two kinds: (1) ignore the weirdo or, to put it a more forgiving way, sensitively avoid intrusion – 'Don't point; don't be rude';

(2) feel provoked, sometimes to aggression, sometimes by an instinct to help or protect.

Occasionally, children are better at ignoring Joe than adults. At the top of the stairs to the slide in the swimming pool the crocodile queue is content to slither past. If he's not part of the game, leave him be, they seemed to reason, being flexible at that age about what constitutes proper behaviour, and so finding him less of an affront to their norms.

So once in a while when a well-intentioned adult butts in, escorting her own angel, she becomes a giant of moral authority among the little people and with all that bulk stops the queue in its tracks.

'The little boy first! Let the little boy go first!'

Joe himself could easily be sidestepped. It's because he's such an insouciant obstacle, careless of the swimming pool code, breaking the rhythm, beyond rules, suddenly dozily indifferent to what we think is pleasure, that he seems to incite attention. There must be something wrong, so we prod him. This is not what little boys do; he's broken down so fix him, nudge him, make him work again like the rest of us. Paradoxically, it's being different but unobtrusive that causes greatest provocation to strangers. The ranting drunk in the marketplace seeks an audience while watching people turn their backs. When Joe takes a quietly eccentric path of his own, he won't be left alone for long. Loud difference scatters the crowds; quiet difference incites them. Tantrums in Sainsbury's clear the aisles; strange placidity in the playground invites bullies. I remember one boy who wanted Joe to go with him down a wide bouncy slide but finding Joe dull and unresponsive at the top, wrapped an arm round his neck and hauled him head-first to the bottom, Joe tumbling, terrified, crying hopelessly where he landed in the ball pit, the little boy scampering off. His mother wanted to know what on earth I thought I was doing, bringing so incapable a child to such a place.

On other occasions, offended by his stolidity, little children hit or push him for a reaction. I can see how Joe's ability to make others feel invisible through guileless indifference causes offence. There are times when he seems not to care whether you or anyone else in the outside world exists. 'Look at me, look at me,' says the child. Joe hears not and sees not, though only for so long. Then he gets upset.

'Are you all right, little boy?' says the lady on the slide.

Joe gazes into the middle distance. Though I feel a mischievous urge to watch the scene unfold, watch as adult conviction, adult norms and expectations collide with the immovable, apparently irrational blob that is Joe's oddness, it's time for me warily to intervene.

The potential for things to go wrong like this, for language to fail, comes from Joe's inability to judge intention, one of the critical facets of our language instinct. The lady means well, and most of us recognise what a well-meaning person sounds like. We're generally exceptionally good at guessing motivation – at least where there is no deliberate deception, and even then we're no pushover. Indeed, whenever we describe communication we imply some sort of state of mind: laughter considered only from the outside, for example, only by what passes on the surface, is merely a distinctive sound, a bit like a saw. But when we say 'he laughed', we mean far more than that he made a strange noise, for we've judged his mood and his intention too.

The philosopher Mary Midgley says the noise alone means nothing, and on the contrary: 'someone who has not had this noise made at him at all, but has been treated with complete outward courtesy and perfectly suppressed smiles, can still have every justification for saying "they were all laughing at me" and can be right'.

If we want to understand such notions as laughter, she says, or indeed anger, tears, smiles, winks, grunts and so on, there is no substitute for grasping the underlying subjective, conscious state of mind from which they all emanate. That is arresting, for it implies that in order to understand language, we need to be able, in a modest way, to mind-read. When Joe sees me wink, he watches a man close one eye to no purpose. Without a sense of what I mean by a wink, of my underlying consciousness, he can't make sense of the gesture. Critical to our understanding of what others mean is a sense that they are conscious beings with intentions. This is at least as important to communication as the literal meaning of the language.

'Are you all right? Do you want to go down the slide?' I see her asking and pointing.

If Joe is paying the least attention, this kind of gentle pestering might, before long, set him off. I feel a small knot of urgency in my chest, wondering how wrong this could go, and I'm out of the pool – hoping Joe doesn't choose the moment to change his mind and launch himself down the slide – and by now into the 'not running really' poolside trot.

'Is something the matter?' asks the moral authority, but Joe has no idea that she intends him a kindness, takes no clue from the earnest anxiety in her voice, or at least, if he does, takes the wrong one, for it turns out to be a question too far, and here it comes, Joe's 'no':

'NnAGH!'

'It's all right, Joe!' I call, unheard above the jangle of echoing voices in the pool. In common with many autistic children, Joe's words can lack proper volume control: 'yes' might be virtually inaudible, 'no' can thunder in response to the most timid inquiry. 'A touch disproportionate, Joe, don't you think?' I want to say as he roars my head off. Somewhat put out by this dose of Joe's ferocity, the good lady on the slide nevertheless feels a duty to persist.

'Do you want to go down the stairs?'

'NnnnnnAGH!' – This time with a lifting screech.

What does she do when every option is contradicted? When offered baked beans, Joe hears the words 'baked beans' but has no sense that they're being suggested rather than imposed and so hears this option as a threat. When the woman on the slide bends towards him with raised eyebrows, he'll probably be picking out one or two words – slide, stairs, for example – but most words and some whole phrases will be unrecognisable. So it is not that he fears or resents the options she puts – he probably can't make any sense of them – rather that he fears and resents her simply as a stranger and her benign tone is no help to her, being no clue to Joe of her good intentions. He has no idea from her words alone whether she means him help or harm.

She winces. 'Is there someone with you?' – reaching out to touch his shoulder and scanning the pool.

'NnnnnnnnnAGHHH!' flapping away her hand, turning heads and with a frantic shaking of his own.

By now I'm barging my own apologetic way up the steps: 'It's all right, he's OK!' I call ahead. 'He's OK, don't worry, he's fine just there.' Well, he's fine just being there, being Joe, it's just that others aren't fine with him just being there.

'Oh, is your daddy here?' Once ready to impose order, now anxious for rescue she feels her merciful moment has turned more militant than could ever have been predicted.

'NnnnnnnnAGGGHHHH!' screams Joe, reaching a pitch of desperation, and the first slap to his own face.

When gentle solicitation fails, there follows either withered embarrassment, smooth social confidence sloughing off in a heap, or something more resentful. 'Well, stuff you!' the affronted expressions seem to say. Joe forfeits his right to their concern for failing to cooperate with their expectations, the stubborn little shit, careless of the decent instincts of decent people. And so, compassion rebuffed, perplexed huff fills in. 'Sod the little boy who's first; you go down, darling.'

I don't blame them; I wish they'd take that view sooner, before Joe, now hot, miserable and bristling defensively, decides to smack one on the little angel. She, shivering and bewildered, does as she's told, her own awkward moral confusion swept away in a rush of flailing limbs and water.

Our language instinct depends on a feeling for tone of voice at least as much as it does on one for literal meaning, and tone derives from our intentions. Goodwill is not evident from words alone and we are rightly suspicious if fine words seem at odds with a careless manner. Sarcasm, humour, impatience, resignation, bitterness, as well as tenderness; any mood or emotion you care to name depends on what we guess from tone of voice to be the 'true' intention of the speaker. Between Jeremy Paxman's 'Yes' and David Frost's is all the difference in the world. I'm fond of the joke that two of the most aggressive phrases in the English language are 'sorry', pronounced with a lingering sneer and the implied parentheses 'how ridiculous your sense of offence is, you small-minded whinger', and the deeply affronted version of 'excuse me!' ('so you think I'm in the wrong?!'). So heavy with irony, these are the kind of apologies that throw down a gauntlet. The occasional error aside, we measure tone, like intention, correctly across a wide range of subtle inflexions. Yet here is a child who seems to mistake pity for aggression. Where perfect pitch is the norm, Joe is tone deaf.

On another occasion, Joe, Cait and I were sitting in the house when Joe, playing with a wooden brick, flung it at his sister, catching her smartly on the shoulder. At once there was swirl of emotional reaction. Cait cried. I was first anxious for her then angry with him. Joe laughed.

I was cross and wanted him to see it, wanted him to understand that his action was wrong, but his giggles rose to hysteria with my temper. How funny the man looks, he must have said to himself. True, Joe had no understanding of the content of my words, but he had no understanding of my very visible mood either. If I summoned more ferocity, he laughed the louder and chucked another wooden brick at his sister to make Daddy do it again. I was at such a loss to know how to put a stop to this that I hit him hard on the hand.

How do you convey disapproval when anger is taken for encouragement? More volume from me seemed to make no difference either. I assume he took it for more excited acclamation. 'Crikey, the audience is lapping this one up.' All I could think of at the time, if I was thinking at all, was that I had to associate his actions with something that stopped him repeating them, some quick consequence he didn't like. Poor Joe. It must have been baffling: 'the man makes funny faces whenever I do this happy thing, so I do it again and out of the blue he hits me'. I'm not sure if even that made much difference, since he would have struggled to work out what the smack had in common with the throwing. Given that throwing often wins approval (throwing stones into the sea, for example, which he enjoys), how can I distinguish exactly the character of his offence? The smack must feel cruelly impulsive and arbitrary.

He stopped after one more brick some short while later, but who knows whether with any sense that it was wrong, despite Cait's tears. My anger only registered with him when it came with some physical consequence, but might still have seemed to be entirely without context. Emotional chastisement didn't work because Joe had such a weak sense of my emotional state, even though I was visibly angry – for anger, reduced to facial expression alone, becomes comic, as we see when children laugh if we merely pretend to be angry with them.

According to child development psychologists, babies are more fascinated by human faces than by anything else. They can distinguish happy faces from sad ones. They can imitate faces. If you stick out your tongue to a very young baby, it will copy you. Paul Bloom, psychology professor at Yale, is impressed: 'These babies have never looked in a mirror, so they have to know instinctively that the tongue they are looking at corresponds to that thing in their mouths that they have never seen before.' He says that before reaching twelve months babies can attend to the emotions of others: 'if babies are crawling toward an area that might be dangerous and an adult makes a horrified or disgusted face, babies know enough to stay away ... by their first birthday babies are social beings'.

Joe, of course, does nothing of the kind even now unless I can communicate to him some cognitive understanding that harm will result. When he wanders from the kitchen with a carving knife in hand, I try to persuade him it's a bad idea not with a shriek or any other sign of alarm, but with a quietly spoken: 'Knife, ouch, Joe. Knife ouch,' and gently take it from him with the silent prayer that he doesn't try in that moment to snatch it away and send the blade windmilling between us. Of course, that doesn't work either, since he struggles to imagine without direct experience how the knife could cause pain. My hopeful calculation is that I stand a marginally better chance with an appeal to logic than to his emotional understanding of facial expressions or tones of voice. If he was inclined to touch something revolting – the poo he occasionally trailed through the house because for some odd reason he felt more comfortable going in his pants that day, for example – I had to restrain him physically; a pained expression, disgusted attitude or tone of voice wouldn't do.

'Poo, Joe. Don't touch. Urgh! Dirty. In toilet, Joe, not pants.' As I hold back his hand.

'Poooo,' he says.

'Yes, Joe. Horrid. Leave poo. Poo in toilet, Joe.'

'Poooo.'

The words of disgust are probably meaningless to him, and yet disgust is one of the most powerful of human emotions. Much as I might feel it, and express it, Joe wouldn't care. And I think of those childcare experts who would have me lavish praise on Joe for his creativity, and wonder how exactly I'd manage the distinction in logic in a way Joe could understand, between creativity and hygiene. Naturally, I don't try.

The human skill for looking at one another and working out what's going on behind the eyes as a swift shortcut to understanding what motivates our words or actions is one of the earliest we develop. One writer and researcher on autism, Uta Frith, calls it 'mentalising'. Simon Baron-Cohen, a psychopathologist at Cambridge who has done so much to open up our understanding of autism, calls the absence of this skill 'mind-blindness', an inability to see that others have minds of their own or work out what's going on inside them (more recently, he's adopted the more familiar term 'empathy'). The rest of us have a yearning to attribute intention to almost everything, animate and inanimate alike. If we compare 'mind-blind' Joe – who seems to attribute intention so erroneously, if at all – with other children's innate capacity for this kind of low-grade mind-reading, we begin to see how critical for normally functioning humanity is our emotional sociability, and we begin to understand how debilitating it is when that sense is impaired.

Alison Gopnik, a psychologist, has imagined how ordinary human behaviour might appear to someone with autism.

This is what it's like to sit at the dinner table. At the top of my field of vision is a blurry edge of nose, in front are waving hands. Around me bags of skin are draped over chairs and stuffed into pieces of cloth, they shift and protrude in different ways. Two dark spots near the top of them swivel relentlessly back and forth. A hole beneath the spots fills with food and from it come a stream of noises. Imagine that the noisy skin bags suddenly move towards you and their noises grew loud, and you have no idea why, no way of explaining them or predicting what they would do next.

That's an extreme state that I think Joe has been lucky to avoid; he's not so severely detached, and over time I think he has also acquired a cognitive understanding of some facial expressions and tones of voice, as opposed to an intuitive one; this capacity grows, but only through the slow growth of association, only when facial expressions come accompanied over and over again by the kind of immediate practical consequences that help him interpret what he sees and hears. Helped by such supplementary evidence, he can establish a correlation: smiles lead to fun, frowns to noisy reprimand. I suspect there's a severe limit to the range of subtler shades of mood and intention he can learn to recognise this way.

In an account in *The New York Times*, neurologist Oliver Sacks describes the remarkable Temple Grandin, a highly intelligent woman who was diagnosed autistic in childhood and now has a Ph.D. in agricultural science. She has also written her own compelling autobiography.

Grandin, says Sacks, had built up a library of experiences which she replayed in her mind like videos: 'She would … learn, by degrees, to correlate what she saw, so that she could then predict how people in similar circumstances might act. She had complemented her experience by constant reading, including reading of trade journals and the *Wall Street Journal* – all of which enlarged her knowledge of the species. "It's a strictly logical process," she explained.'

For most of us, these are clearly skills we are born to acquire, blessed with an astonishing facility to learn them and requiring none of the laborious analysis that Grandin still finds necessary.

In another experiment described by Paul Bloom, a small remote-controlled robot is sent towards a three-year-old. The child's parent stands to one side pretending to be terrified, making fearful expressions and sounds. Normally developing children take the hint and keep away; autistic children show no fear.

Joe's smarting hand, Cait's tears and my guilt illustrate that this absence of a sense of tone and intention in language is a costly, exhausting, frustrating shame, consistent with Joe's general inability to read and understand emotional expression with a full sense of what it implies.

It's unquestionably true that dogs often do better. In *Not Even Wrong*, a book on his son's autism, Paul Collins describes a guide-dog training centre based in an open prison in the United States. Inmates on the Liberty Dog Training Program – yes, seriously – prepare dogs to work with, among others, autistic children. The dogs' main function is to offer companionship to people with autism who find animals easier to get on with than people. They also warn of danger – from traffic, for example. Next, they interpret tone of voice and intention. Their great advantage, says Collins, is that dogs know when someone is trying to be friendly or threatening and people with autism often don't.

If it's true that communication makes sense only when we impute a state of mind to the speaker or imagine an emotion behind the expression, and if it's true that dogs are quite good at understanding human communication, does that mean dogs have a sense of our consciousness? According to the developmental psychologist Paul Bloom recent studies suggest that dogs outperform chimps on many tasks involving social reasoning, presumably, he speculates, because they hunt in packs.

We all have moments of doubt, we all get it wrong sometimes – 'are you laughing with me or at me?' – but I'm struck by how spectacularly wrong Joe can be, not wrong by degrees, but diametrically wrong: how he'll respond to sadness with violence and can treat distress so lightly that if a thump or two frees him from inconvenience, he'll dish them out liberally; how he can greet a smile with menace, and recoil fearfully from a gesture of surprise or gentle solicitation. Watching fear flood his face when nothing threatening is said or implied is itself terrifying.

In the swimming pool, at the top of the slide that day, I picked him up, mumbled an explanation to the poor woman who'd just seen her compassion end with a wailing child thumping himself, feeling for some reason that it is she who is owed the apology (a sincere 'sorry' this time), and we worked our way back down the narrow steps. Behind us, the normal bustle of normal children's normal behaviour resumed as soon as we were out of the way.

I carried him for a while before he wriggled down to the floor and I followed as he made his way over to a bench at one end of the pool, piled with other swimmers' fluffy towels. He sat beneath the clock with the double-ended second-hand, inclined to help himself to a towel, but making do with the warmth from me instead.

We behave as if Joe's emotional register is like ours. We expect to reach into it with casual ease, the way we reach into the minds of everyone else. We deploy a kind of anthropomorphism. Strange to call it that, I know, when Joe looks like one of us already. Surely his instincts will be broadly like ours, his preferences and thought processes too. When his actions resemble ours, we assume he acts for the same reasons. If he hits, we guess that it is antagonism or aggression. We barely stop to wonder whether that action has the same significance for him as it would for us.

Why does he do it? What possible attraction is there sitting, dripping, cold, expressly not doing the thing you came to do, the thing all others desire? But if we feel the least bit mystified, think of the purposeless chaos, the bottomless mystery seen through his eyes, as people talk, grimace, move about, often apparently without agency, often without much fathomable intention. For Joe, the insane, the unpredictable world exists outside.

After the incident on the slide, he's not interested in the pool any more and sits on the bench for a minute or two longer. No, he doesn't want to go back in the water; no, he doesn't want any more slide; no, but quietly and with touching gentleness, he doesn't want to watch the other children. We walk back to the door at the top of the stairs to the changing rooms, Joe with his hands up by his chin and arms pressed to his chest, torn between seeking a hand to steady himself over the wet tiles and the reflex to hug himself to keep warm, and we go home.

Within a couple more weeks at school, Joe's head-banging

began to decline. Just once more he seems to have tapped his brow unconvincingly against a soft covering on the wall and then largely given up a strategy that hurt perhaps too much with too little pay-off. Or perhaps he just felt he was beginning to be understood.

The staff at school worked hard to interpret him, his sounds and his moods. With all their human sophistication they learnt to decipher his strange emotional vocabulary and maybe he learnt a little of theirs. Even if he remained at a loss as to how to interpret their tone, he began to know and cease to fear their routine. Here was the first sign of progress, and as the weeks passed I began at last to fear less for the consequences at school of simple questions. At school, as at home, he still says no, often. I still admire, sort of, the conviction. Above all, I hope that, somehow, love can be heard even by a tin ear.

# 5
# Intention

Here was the new regime: every other weekend Joe came home, collected on Friday at 11am, returned on Sunday at 4pm. Before he went to Bristol, no child had been capable of a more insistently, perpetually in-your-face presence than Joe. Miss him though we did, his presence now was no more than part of life's punctuation, often intermittent: the intermittence of a klaxon, true enough, and still the same old commanding presence the minute he was with us, but with eerie and silent interludes.

How would he react, I wondered, when I collected him from his mother's house. He was waiting at the living-room window, saw me walk up the path, zipped round to stand in the hall and was ready as the door swung open:

'Pak!' (pasta), he said.

'Hello, Joe!'

'Pak!'

His weekends at home soon found a new rhythm, much like the old. We settled into it and with the slickness that comes of familiarity slid quickly through the days into Sunday afternoon, and the journey back to school. He was mostly well behaved at this time, late October darkening into November, subdued but good, passing the time with an unusual tranquillity that incited in me a fidget of second thoughts about whether he couldn't stay at home after all, thoughts I dismiss for the time being and set off for school anyway. That's what we do now, we get on with it.

That is, we move with syrupy slovenliness into the journey, through two zombie hours or more on the motorway, taking in our now ritual stop for a ritual seat by the window of the same service station and the same ritually vile chips, coated and fried in that customary chemical broth. Joe devours them. In the car next to me, he also steadily devours his standard four tangerines, a packet of the usual crisps and the plate of peanut butter sandwiches he often brings for company, if not always to eat.

We play the tape of *Abba's Greatest Hits* that Joe had clasped in both hands when we left the house. I've been warned that it has become mandatory listening. We play it continuously and would play only the track 'SOS' if Joe had his way, which, I find myself idly calculating at just under four minutes (rewinding included) would entertain us approximately thirty-three times before Bristol.

> *… When you're near me darling,*
> *Can't you hear me,*
> *SOS!*
> *And the love you gave me …*

I can't decide whether the song is audible sponge cake, the softest ever, or a work of pop genius. As we drum along the M4 to relentless Abba, I'm struck again by the arbitrariness of this turn in Joe's life amid so much clockwork; the day we first brought him to Bristol his hour must have struck thirteen.

At these moments, routine helps avoid uncomfortable questions: ignore the elephant on the back seat of the mind and just drive; that way argument can be put aside. For Joe, by contrast, quite brutally, there never was argument. What I daren't do – sink into contemplation of ifs and buts – I suspect Joe cannot do, and so while I seek the absent mindedness of routine as a way of negotiating this moment, Joe cannot but depend on it for his normal compass.

> *… I don't know how but I suddenly lose control*
> *There's a fire within my soul*
> *Just one look and I can hear a bell ring*
> *One more look and I forget everything, o-o-o-oh*
> *Mama Mia …*

And yet, as I drive, concentrate though I might on getting on with it, one glance at him is all it takes to unstop the speculative thoughts about his thoughts. It comes unbidden to us, this prying into the mental life of others, and my head aches to conceive Joe's existence, as I imagine it, in an intellectual nutshell, lacking even the knowledge that depth, argument and understanding exist, largely unaware that others have a mental life at all. Like the futile effort to imagine the state of death, I sense the impossibility of sharing such an unearthly perspective. How do you ponder deeply the absence of reflective thought? I think of the hours the rest of us spend every day in calculation, consideration, understanding the normal motivations of life lived amid others, and picture such thoughts whistling past Joe's lonesome consciousness. So much, in my case, for the bulwark of routine, which is nagged to pieces by instinctive questions.

For we need to stare deeper into the sink that is Joe's mind-blindness. It involves a failure fully to understand not just speech – the speech of well-meaning ladies in swimming pools, to take one example – but another failure already hinted at, the failure to understand a great deal of behaviour too, the behaviour of adults who take him from a familiar place and plant him in an alien one, to take another.

The bitter consequence for Joe is this: in the world he observes, much human action has had meaning rinsed out. The quality that makes other people's behaviour intelligible, the fact that it is done for a reason – imperfect, irrational, selfish, self-defeating, nasty, hasty though reason and action may sometimes be – the fact that what we do is in our own minds at least the servant of some intention, has been substantially washed from his conception of life. He fully grasps what we intend neither from what we say, nor from what we do. Let's be clear, this need not be due to lack of intelligence; it is quite specifically a lack of ability to work out what other people think they are up to – in this present case, the reasons for bundling him into the car and returning him to school.

I believe that Joe exists within the veneer of thought, rarely penetrating, not strictly through any incapacity for thought or reason, rather from his inability to see that I have a thinking, reasoning consciousness of my own.

So though we had our reasons for sending him to a residential school, none was meaningful or communicable to Joe. He sits next to me, sometimes chirpy, sometimes singing to himself or laughing irresistibly, sometimes quiet, at times sad, sometimes holding the hand I rest on the gearstick, all the while an ocean apart. What sense does he make of it all? Precious little, I guess. It must seem random, pointless, inexplicable. One day I live there, the next they put me here. Events come along, no point, no reason.

He's laughing now, out of the blue, bent by spasms of giggles, then relaxing into an expression of pure mischief, about what I'll never know, though who cares if only this mood would see the day out.

> … *Take a chance, take a chance*
> *Take a chaka-chan-chance.*
> *If you change your mind,*
> *I'm the first in line*
> *Honey I'm still free …*

Children packed off to boarding school are at least told it's doing them good. Disagree though they might, they're offered a reason. Joe in this respect is less like the reluctant boarder than a diminutive Joseph K from Kafka's *Trial*: he doesn't know and never could understand the case against him. In *The Trial*, the reader's sense that society should function through cause and effect, through behaviour based on motives and reasons, rebels against a mysterious case lacking all evidence. For Joe, other people's behaviour must often have the flavour of absurdity; the wonder is he rebels so seldom.

And so to his imagined question: 'Mummy, Daddy – Mee and Dee – what's it all about, this business of a new school?' I can make, to his mind, no meaningful answer. It is beyond explanation. Moreover, he would never expect one; he would never think to ask. As far as Joe can see, precious little lies beneath the surface of my actions, for when it comes to other people surface is often all there is. To find an answer would be to know my motivation, and motivation is a concept belonging in my psychology, a psychology he seems to conceive only in fragments, if at all. In the trial of our Joe, from his point of view, there is no case, simply a world of instant verdicts known only when sentence is carried out. Sending him away must be one example among thousands daily that the world is arbitrary in the extreme.

Joe's surprisingly patient bewilderment at this despotic state of affairs invites a question: how do the rest of us make sense of the human activity raging about us? The short answer is that we are, as he is not, instinctive mind-readers who supply motivation to almost everything we see.

Our antennae are normally remarkably well tuned to other people's intentions. Such is this knack of ours for guessing other people's inner experience that the psychologist Nicholas

Humphrey has described it as our defining characteristic, and names us '*Homo psychologicus*'. We are, he says, born psychologists:

> Human beings ... had to become sensitive to other people's moods and passions, appreciative of their waywardness or stubbornness, capable of reading the signs in their faces and equally the lack of signs, capable of guessing what each person's past experience holds hidden in the present for the future. They had above all to make sense of the ghost in the machine.

The philosopher Daniel Dennett writes similarly:

> We use folk psychology all the time to explain and predict each other's behaviour; we attribute beliefs and desires to each other and with confidence – and quite unselfconsciously – and spend a substantial portion of our waking lives formulating the world – not excluding ourselves – in these terms ... it is a theory of great generative power and efficiency. For instance, watching a film with a highly original and un-stereotyped plot, we see the hero smile at the villain and we all swiftly and effortlessly arrive at the same complex theoretical diagnosis: 'Aha!' we conclude (but perhaps not consciously). 'He wants her to think he doesn't know she intends to defraud her brother.'

Is he right? Can we really, reliably presume to know what other people are thinking?

We're all aware of occasions when we've misjudged others, perhaps because, as Ludwig Wittgenstein said, there is no means of objective verification, and thus another person's consciousness is ultimately unknowable. It is, he argued, a beetle in a box:

> Suppose everyone had a box with something in it: we call it a 'beetle'. No one can look into anyone else's box, and everyone says he knows what a beetle is only by looking at *his* beetle. – Here it would be quite possible for everyone to have something different in his box. One might even imagine such a thing constantly changing.

Wittgenstein didn't mean his metaphor to be used in this way, but it works; I can never know for sure if your beetle is like mine. Yet for all practical purposes we assume otherwise, that our beetles are much alike, and this subjective tendency passes a practical test. Dennett and Humphrey do not propose an infallible mechanism, but one usually so dependable that we wince on the rare occasions it fails us.

But philosophy isn't done with us, and has another hurdle to place in the way of folk psychology. It is overwhelmingly the view of philosophers and neuropsychologists that there is, there can be, no ghost in the machine. The intellectual fashion in the study of philosophy of mind is materialist, and our perception of a ghost, alive and well and very much in charge, is held to be merely an illusion. How could there be such stuff as consciousness, seeming to exist independently of matter, they ask, and yet also having sensory awareness of matter as it registers the world beyond us and even, in the movement of our own limbs, able to control matter? Is it separate and different, or not? It is not, they say: consciousness must be material and there is no separate and immaterial ghost.

In an odd way, Joe takes them at their word. Research published in 2004 from the University of Washington used brain scans to suggest that people with autism look at faces as if they were objects, people as if they were machines. Normal adults use a separate part of the brain to process faces and objects; those with autism usually don't seem to distinguish between the two, treating faces in the same fashion as cars, excepting only their mothers'. I sometimes imagine Joe as a scientist who looks upon any human scene, and in order to understand what is going on around him, without resorting to such debunked notions as ghosts in the machine, has to calculate the movement of every single particle, plot its course and, under known laws, determine how one particle will affect another and so how the scene will unfold. Of course, he fails; our illogical perceptions serve us far better.

It matters not for our purposes whether our psychological sense of a commanding self-consciousness is an illusion; the perception remains a far more effective shortcut to an understanding of what's going on in other people than doing the materialist calculation properly. The psychologist Paul Bloom says we are all, psychologically speaking, instinctive upholders of the separation of a ghostly mind from a material body, paid-up Cartesian dualists, whatever the view of science and philosophy of mind. If the materialists are right, it is, as the philosopher Galen Strawson points out, a fact that our instinct finds impossible to accept, one of those beliefs that are completely involuntary for us, that cannot be deflected by reason or argument. We can see something of the extent to which the rest of us depend on this extraordinary and deeply ingrained human capacity, this audacious presumption about other people's thoughts and intentions, whether logically fallible or not, by watching what happens in someone who lacks it, someone who appears to act as Wittgenstein would require: Joe. So banal has this talent become to most of us, that when we find such an example we glimpse a mind of mythical curiosity.

While reading one evening, when Joe was about seven, I came across a Chinese proverb: 'The wise man points to the moon; the fool looks at the finger.' An awful unwelcome knowing, a hateful, hard-hearted truth, set me musing about where Joe would look if I pointed to the moon. I half knew already, and sat vacant for ten minutes.

A few nights later in a strange spirit of masochistic fatalism, I took him out on a clear evening. The moon was about half full, bright and attention-seeking in the night sky. We stepped onto the front lawn where Joe, at a loss to what was in store for him following this unusual excursion from routine, waited for the next move.

'Hey, look, Joe!' I say, and point. 'The moon. Beautiful ... Joe, look!'

He turns to my voice, sees me with arm raised, and looks away.

'Yes, yes,' his disdainful expression suggests, 'but what are we doing here? What's next? Car? Mummy? Swimming? Shop? Resume a routine I know, if you please.'

'Joe, Joe, up there, Joe. Look up! Up, Joe! The moon.'

He turns again to look at me, silently ignores the arm, which he's already judged pointless, and looks away again.

'Nagh!'

I walk over and try to lift his chin, still pointing: 'Up, Joe, look up!'

But his eyes are like water in a glass and swivel stubbornly horizontal, earth-bound. He wriggles free.

'Naagh!'

I turn over my left hand, stretch out its index finger, watch the thumb instinctively unfold, linger over the shape and see that the lesson is crueller still. For the proverbial fool is halfway there: when he looks at the finger, he understands at least that the finger is the purpose of the hand's contortion. His attention is informed, if ultimately wrong. My son seems to know not even this. I have no idea if it's the finger he noticed, or the whole hand, or some part of it, or the arm. My pointing hand did not, for him, have any obvious significance, not in the pointing finger's direction, not even in the finger. What does Joe think when he sees me point? 'This man moves his arm, puts his hand into an odd shape,' I guess, using Occam's razor to ill-effect: the simplest explanation being that what is placed most immediately in front of you is the intended object of attention. But the pointed finger, of course, by convention, by necessity, is not itself the point. It's supposed to refer, to direct elsewhere, not to keep us here but to lead our attention over there. How can I lead Joe's gaze along the invisible line from my fingertip to that somewhere? A thing perceived in isolation with no relevance to the rest of creation communicates nothing. It is a signpost aimed at itself. Unless information shifts us from one place to another, connects here with there, this with that, so what? Alone and irrelevant, inert, uninteresting, the pointing finger is only its senseless self. Thus the big struggle with Joe, to find a way of acquainting him with the simplest of notions: that the pointing finger points.

We go back inside, out of the cold. In, out, no rhyme, no reason, more absurdity. Poor Joe simply didn't know what I meant. That night, a hard night, I sit for hours, jaws clenched, grinding teeth on piety, feeding rancour in a remembered line from Martin Amis's autobiography as he watched his father Kingsley fume over some cruelty in life, and says how he observed a man 'hating God'.

Joe is no fool, of course. Fool is a word for those we hold in contempt and contempt is altogether inappropriate for Joe's precipitous difficulty. We might feel mystification, or horror, perhaps, but contempt would be the emotion of a fool.

For most of us, the point of pointing is normally transparent. Why? Seeing Joe's mystification it isn't obvious to me from our actions alone that it is at all clear what we're up to with this spontaneous flicking-finger gesture. Something must supplement the movement in order to turn it into understanding and, indeed, *Homo psychologicus* finds it easy. The trick, as we all instinctively know but Joe does not, is to follow the eye and the mind at least as closely as the line of the finger.

The evidence from academic studies of autism is slightly ambiguous. It suggests, contrary to my night on the lawn with Joe, that autistic children do understand gestures designed to make them perform a task, so-called instrumental gestures such as beckoning or a finger pressed to the lips for quiet. But researchers have also found that these children lack a critical ability known as shared or joint attention. This is the common tendency to look where another is looking or pointing and to take cues from the attitude of these other observers. The striking thing about this (it is easily observed in parents and normal young children) is that the children are interested not only in the object pointed to, but what the adult thinks about it, and seem capable of absorbing this unspoken feeling. It's a behaviour also known as social referencing. Children typically glance first at the face, then at the hand. In other words, children following a pointed finger are also mind-reading, identifying an object and simultaneously understanding the parent's attitude towards it.

Shared attention, which depends on facial signals of emotion, is absent in children with autism. Simon Baron-Cohen screened thousands of children aged eighteen months, including a test for shared attention, that is whether the children paid heed to the parent's gaze. By forty-two months nearly every child who had failed the tests was diagnosed with autism. Attempting to play the Chinese wise man, I hoped to convey wonder at the moon, and failed. The wonder is that the rest of you would know how I felt from a jutting digit and a tone of voice.

Joe does now respond perfectly well to the instruction 'point to' – provided, obviously, that he also recognises and understands the name of the thing to which you've asked him to point – but he had to be laboriously taught. For many months we ground through a teaching programme that involved coercing him into jabbing at pictures or objects as we named them, initially by holding his finger and doing it for him. His hand, index finger crooked, now gestures easily towards the picture in the book that you're after.

'Point to the sheep, Joe.'

'Peep,' he says, pointing correctly.

But Joe knows his own intentions – and his own pointed finger has an objective that he already understands. When the rest of us point something out to Joe, I suspect he's lucky if he grasps half our meaning, and if it's argued that he sometimes points voluntarily, we soon see that this is usually to get something he wants, it is instrumental, an action with a machine-like effect: namely, Daddy sorts it. His pointing is not to share any feeling, for how could he, when it seems there is no other mind with which to share?

Full-grown chimpanzees in the wild compare well on many skills with human infants, but do not point. Attempts to teach them have not been altogether successful. Clearly, pointing is not the trivial skill we assume it to be, but part of a sophisticated social repertoire, exploiting the capacity for mind-reading that makes us qualitatively superior communicators.

Being mindful of Joe's inability to discern intention, I began to think I could anticipate its effects, but so pervasively do we deploy these mentalising skills, this knack for guessing the thoughts and intentions of others, that he surprised me on countless mundane occasions. At home, I'd sometimes drift into the kitchen to make myself a sandwich. Coming in after me and seeing the cheese filling, Joe would object:

'Nnaghh!'

His assumption seems to be that any sandwich made is a sandwich made for him. Now there are at least two explanations for making a sandwich: I want a sandwich and intend it for me, or someone else wants a sandwich. Joe understands cause and effect well enough. If I push this button here, the tape will play. If I tip this cup, the milk will flow onto the carpet. If I hit Caitlin, Dee makes funny faces.

Understanding desire is harder, ranking in difficulty somewhere between mechanical cause and effect and the monstrous problem of deciphering human intention. Joe's instinct is to assume that only he wants, that only he is capable of wanting. Only through patient explanation does he begin to see that the world might be otherwise, a lesson he then seems to forget easily. And so if he doesn't want, what's going on? We can only guess his reasoning:

'What's this? A sandwich. A *cheese* sandwich? But I don't want a cheese sandwich. Dee, the thing that makes things for me, must be malfunctioning. Why is Dee making a sandwich when I don't want one? It will be given to me as all sandwiches made for me are given to me. This must be stopped. I shall say so:

'Nnaghh!'

What someone else might want wouldn't be an instinctive question, for Joe doesn't presume that they want, full stop. I don't mean that they 'don't want anything for the time being, thank you', that they're satisfied just now; I mean that they never want, never have wants, unless those wants are clearly, precisely articulated.

'Not for you, Joe.'

'Naaggh!'

'It's for me.'

'Ngaaagh!'

'Sandwich for Daddy.'

A blank look.

'Daddy wants sandwich. Daddy eat sandwich. Joe no sandwich! Daddy sandwich. For Daddy.'

A puzzled look, and then an abrupt loss of interest, at which point calm is restored. Joe, in Joe's world, is unique in being motivated by desires, fears, passions. If he didn't want a sandwich then ordinarily no sandwich could be wanted, and it's a surprise for him to discover otherwise.

Once I'd made my sandwich, another odd thing happened: Joe stood in the way. He saw me walk towards him – there was only one way out of the kitchen and he was in it – but made no movement to step aside, come in properly or turn round and go out. I shifted to one side so that we could edge past one another, as you do. Joe stood still. It wasn't a confrontational stance: on the contrary, he wasn't actively doing anything, just standing there with no sense of what standing still implied. It implied, because I knew where I was going, that I was going to bump into him. Where I was going was obvious to anyone, except Joe. Seeing me walk towards a door, *you* would assume I wanted to go through it. Not so Joe.

We often ran into blackspots of household congestion like this, too often for them to be the result of momentary indecision. It was something he'd do frequently and so, in a spirit of mischievous curiosity, I'd walk right up to him, the two of us standing two inches apart for half a minute while Joe loitered, waiting listlessly for whatever might happen next, mooching, his body a swaying curve of boredom, tummy like a spinnaker, biting on a thumbnail.

Sometimes he seizes the moment for one of his sudden, enveloping bear hugs, and the cheese sandwich has to take its chances somewhere in the middle. I suppose my movement towards him had appeared random and might take me anywhere, might stop at any moment, as in some cases it had to, and so for him to move aside would be a little like trying to avoid snowflakes in a blizzard. I must assume that in his eyes I was just such a swirling snowflake. In order to understand that he was in my path, he would have had to guess where it led and deduced that we were about to collide. To do that he would have needed to make assumptions about my intentions, but as far as he was concerned I had no more intention than the weather.

Which brings out the contrast with the rest of us. For we are so habitually inclined to attribute intention, and act accordingly – not least because it helps anticipate other people's movements – that we often talk of the weather as if it actually knows what it wants: 'The sun is trying to poke through the clouds.' A figure of speech, of course, but an indicative one. The sun isn't 'trying' to do anything, we just find it convenient to talk about it that way.

Indeed, child psychologists report that we are over eager to attribute mental states. If you show a normal young child two shapes moving about on a computer screen which behave like independent, agitated snowflakes, the children don't like it. Random, independent movement when there seems to be the potential for a relationship disappoints them. If one shape appears to be following the same path as the other, however, the children are happier, and interpret what they see in terms of human motivation: 'Look, it's chasing!' They seem to think it's to be expected when even inanimate objects appear to be influenced by each other and thus to express an intention towards one another. This is a powerful, instinctive mode of thought, and yet so familiar to us that we perhaps underestimate the achievement.

'The ability to do psychology,' writes Nicholas Humphrey, 'however much it may nowadays be an ability possessed by every ordinary man and woman, is by no means an ordinary ability. Let no one pretend that natural psychology or psychology under any other title is anything but an extraordinarily difficult thing to do ... it represents the most peculiar and sophisticated development in the evolution of the human mind.'

Simon Baron-Cohen spends several pages of his book *Mindblindness* simply describing everyday examples of natural psychology, to try to wake us up to its ubiquity. It's a hard thought experiment, he says, to imagine life without it: 'When someone points out all this mind-reading to you,' he writes, 'it hits you with some force. Recall the apocryphal man who was shocked to discover he had been speaking in prose all his life. We mind-read all the time, effortlessly, automatically, and mostly unconsciously. That is, we are not even aware we are doing it – until we stop to examine the words and concepts that we are using.'

It is such a habitual, casual habit of mind that we are sub-limely unaware of the complexity of what we attempt every day. Seeing me make a sandwich, you might easily assume that I felt hungry, simple as that. Except that beneath this simplicity is a skill humans possess to a unique degree, and upon which depend many sophisticated social arrangements, much of the love, understanding, cooperation (and competition) which make civilisation possible.

Daniel Dennett offers a familiar case: 'Every time we venture out on the highway, for example, we stake our lives on the reli-ability of our general expectations about the perceptual beliefs, normal desires and decision proclivities of other motorists ...'

When I was a young journalist on a local daily paper, an untidy, haunted-looking man came into the office and I took the call from a grateful receptionist to come through and see him.

'I've got a story that'll blow the lid off local politics,' he said.

'Oh, yes?' I said, as he drew on a cigarette. 'Tell me about it.'

'I hope you can handle something this big …'

'We'll try.'

'OK … Social services are trying to kill me …'

The police kept picking him up, he said, and telling him he was paranoid. 'You'd be paranoid if someone was trying to kill you,' he added with disconcerting logic.

The murderous methods of social services staff were cruel and devious, he went on. Through hypnosis, they were tempting him to drive into the oncoming traffic on the other side of the road.

Trite though it is to say that only someone suicidal or not in their right mind would deliberately steer a car into oncoming traffic, it could not be said to my informant. When we drive, we assume most people in the other lane are not paranoid schizophrenic, or hypnotised, and we drive in the confidence that they are highly unlikely to veer into our path. We assume this, if we give it much thought, because we think they think as we do, and that driving on the wrong side of the road would be a foolish thing to do if you wanted to stay alive. This is a statement of the blindingly obvious, but only, I submit, because we've grown blasé about the psychological presumption on which it rests. At traffic lights, junctions, roundabouts, we assume other drivers will abide by the rules because we have a collective self-interest in doing so. It only seems at all remarkable when we become aware that those with mind-blindness would not be able to make such straightforward calculations. And then the very fact that it is obvious for the rest of us to be able to presume to know what others are thinking becomes amazing.

An odd consequence of Joe's inability to see that my mind has contents, contents which are limited in scope, emotionally constrained, driven by my own purposes, is that I can't say to him 'I don't know.' To know and not to know are states of mind. If, as he assumes, I have no mind, he can't understand that there may be constraints on what's in it. If he asks for something, he seems to assume I will be able to deliver it. If he wants Mummy to arrive, now, he looks to me as if I can conjure her appearance round the corner there and then. If he wants to go swimming with her tomorrow, he expects me to tell him that he may.

'Peep, en ets (sleep, then swimming).'

'I don't know, Joe.'

'Peep, ets.'

'I don't know, Joe, you'll have to ask Mummy.'

'Ets. Ets. Ets, Dee, ets!' Until I phone up to find out.

Now and then I'll endeavour to resign myself to the notion that I am more machine-like to Joe than human, though it's an uncomfortable truth. When he wants something from me, I must suppose that I am nature's universal vending machine, the great button to all desire, which if pressed frequently enough will provide. He credits me with omniscience and omnipotence, which is flattering, but somewhat demanding.

Lacking, to his mind, any mind of my own, I guess that I function as an automatic portal to the world with no gatekeeper, no consciousness in operation, a machine with no ghost imagined or needed.

Recent research suggests that the rest of us second guess other people's thoughts by watching what they do, subconsciously imagining ourselves performing the same task, and then noting how we feel. Narender Ramani and colleagues at Oxford University found that when we watch other people's actions the motor system of our brain lights up in a kind of mental dry run, allowing us to share the physical sense of what they're going through (and hence what they might feel about it) without actually going through it ourselves. These are areas of the brain found to be abnormal in people with autism. Other research has also suggested the existence of so-called mirror cells that replicate a sense in our own minds of what we observe in others.

If it's true that those with mind-blindness like Joe would not be able to imagine the commonsense values and motivations of the drivers of other cars, or predict their actions by performing a mental dry run of their own, why don't they assume that all driver behaviour will be random, a snowstorm of vehicles; why don't they expect a sudden swerve from the far lane into their own at any time? As we blunder down the M4, why isn't Joe in a state of terror at the slabs of HGV hurtling in the opposite direction? The answer is probably that he doesn't expect disaster because so far it has never happened. His judgement is based not on human understanding but on past performance or, in other words, a sense of ritual or routine. Cars do what cars do, though not for any particular reason. This is the critical point: cars are only their reputation, without present purpose: no one is late, no one has relatives to visit, jobs to go to, places to see; rather, they hurtle around as large lumps of red, blue and white, just as such lumps have always hurtled around in Joe's experience. Yes they have people in them, he knows that much, but the people, being machine-like too, follow the rules of all similar machines. Joe never expected a car to hit him – until one did – and he had no idea that being hit by one would hurt – until it did – and now he is afraid of them. As the advertisements for investments are required to say, past performance is no guide to the future. Any student of human affairs knows as much. Joe still seems to expect otherwise.

Thus we find ourselves with an ingrained tool of perception – mind-reading – apparently at odds with the philosophical orthodoxy of Wittgenstein and the materialists, but with remarkable explanatory power. Joe, more respectful of that orthodoxy, less inclined to the perceptual fallacies, is in a state of perpetual bewilderment.

Our mind-reading faculty helps make the world a little less unpredictable, and also helps us learn at prodigious speed – about others as we learn about ourselves and about their views and attitudes to the world around us, views about what's dangerous being but one example. I'll mention just one more. It occurred when Joe, aged three or four, was seated on a tiny chair at a tiny table while a psychologist perched on an equally small chair opposite. Slowly, deliberately, the psychologist produced a clear plastic cylindrical tub with a lid in which there were three holes: round, square and triangular. Parents everywhere will know them. He removed the lid (a mistake), emptied half-a-dozen shaped wooden blocks onto the table and replaced the lid. Next, the obvious test: taking one of the shapes between finger and thumb with the deliberation of a magician, fingers splayed, a dainty touch and a raised eyebrow, he showed us clearly how to push it neatly through the appropriate hole. It clattered into the tub. Presto, he smiled, and pushed the remaining shapes towards Joe.

Joe pulled the whole tub closer, slipped off the lid, which he tossed onto the floor, and began plopping shapes straight in. Less stage-craft, admittedly, and, oh, all right, less precision too, but my, what efficiency!

Only, no, sorry, the psychologist was not testing for that.

'Joe! Joe!' he interrupted through the plonking of blocks. 'Let me show you again.'

Something in the rules of the test forbade spoken instruction. Joe had to watch, learn and repeat. He watched as the man poured out the pieces, which Joe liked, watched as the man demonstrated his magic again, and then repeated exactly what he'd done the first time, flipping off the lid and chucking in the first of the shapes.

'No, Joe,' said the man, taking away the toy.

Joe, however, didn't care for 'no'. He thought 'yes', the pouring out bit was most interesting and he wanted it again. He thought it quite insistently, in fact, and I have to say I agreed, though not perhaps with quite Joe's vehemence, as the two of them became locked in a tussle for control of the tub. I smiled inwardly (memo to myself: conquer this impulse to sly amusement at those caught in Joe's turbulence), impressed by Joe's directness: stuff the prissy malarky with the holes, let's do the noisy, jumbly bit. Joe, meanwhile, was being failed.

His difficulty with the task makes sense to me with hindsight as a partial expression of mind-blindness. He might have been capable of understanding that certain shapes could be passed though certain corresponding holes, I can't recall, but I suspect he hadn't understood that this was what was wanted of him and so did something else, whatever else took his fancy in fact. In order to complete a task, we must have some sense of what the task is and we define that, often as not, by what we think the maker had in mind. How often when we confront a game or puzzle do we say: 'So, what are you supposed to do?' What did the designer of this thing intend to be the object of the game? To Joe, other people's prior intentions are out of bounds.

The bitter implication for Joe of these stories seems to be this: that he is alone in a sense none of us can quite comprehend. Unable to reach out with empathy to others and unable to understand the degrees to which we can and cannot reach him, he lives by trying to impose a grossly imperfect regularity on life, by insisting on routine and familiarity, and by raging with frustration – or subsiding in bafflement – at the mystery of those failed expectations.

The word autism derives from the Greek *autos*, or self. Uta Frith tells us in her now standard account of autism, *Explaining the Enigma*, that the term was first used in psychiatry by Eugen Bleuler at the turn of the nineteenth century in a study of schizophrenia. He described, she says, 'a narrowing of relationships to people and to the outside world, a narrowing so extreme that it seemed to exclude everything except the person's own self.' There is another phrase, 'autistic aloneness', coined by Leo Kanner, who in 1943 published the first account of autism and described the isolation caused by these fierce limits on social capability. That the rest of us are not so alone is perhaps because we are able to believe we can touch the minds of others, share thoughts and emotions, recognise fellow travellers. When we do feel most alone, it is often because we feel most misunderstood, when it is as if there is no correspondence, no echo. In trying to imagine what it is to be mind-blind, to be unable to form a view about the mental state of others, I feel a rush of claustrophobia, a solitariness that fills me with dread.

When I was a small child I indulged a fear – or was it a dream? – that everyone else was a robot and only I alive. As in *The Truman Show*, the Hollywood film of a character whose whole life – adopted as he is by a TV mogul – takes place in a purposefully constructed film set of utopian suburbia, they say (dystopian we think), for the benefit of a prime-time audience, the point of my imagined uniqueness was to see how a creature, strange and miraculous as I, lived and behaved, and so hidden cameras that I could never detect spied on my every movement.

Excepting the titanic vanity of my fantasy, is this Joe's world too? Is he, in his own mind, the point of it all, with all his internal reflections, thoughts, motives just about all the thoughts and reflections there are? If so, though he would never stop to reflect on that fact, he would be the only boy in the world. And the rest of us? The rest of us ... just are. Relatively empty of emotional content, we move, we function, we cause him difficulty, force him to do strange things, facilitate his desires, or not, come and go and make strange noises.

I have to acknowledge that, agonise as I do whether or not Joe has very much capacity for empathy, many people who know him are firmly convinced that he has, and that I am too doubting. His mother says she can give dozens of examples, but perhaps none better than when, after Joe had been a long time under general anaesthetic with the doctors struggling to bring him round, they asked her into the recovery room and she whispered into his ear: 'Joe, it's Mummy.' He opened his eyes and stretched out his arms for her to hug him. She doesn't believe that she is a machine to him, excepting those occasions when there's a whiff of video and obsession outweighs empathy.

It was once believed that all children, not just those with autism, lacked the ability to 'de-centre,' as it is known among educationalists, to picture the world from some point of view different from their own. Children as old as six or seven were thought to be so egocentric that they couldn't imagine what objects looked like from another angle. Jean Piaget, whose powerful influence cemented this view, showed children a model of a range of three mountains of different colours, one with snow on top, one with a house and one with a red cross. A doll was then placed at some position away from the child and the child was asked to select the doll's view from a range of pictures. Children find this task hard even up to the age of eight or nine. Piaget concluded that they were incapable of imagining the world from another perspective. But he was mistaken, his test was flawed.

More recent tests by other researchers have presented children with a model of two walls intersecting like a cross. The children are asked where they should hide within the model in order that someone else in another position – a playmate who is trying to find them, say – won't be able to see them. They are able to work out perfectly easily which areas of the model the playmate has sight of from any given position, and in which areas they can safely hide. It is impossible to reconcile this experiment with the notion that children are incapable of imagining what others see.

In fact, according to the developmental psychologist Margaret Donaldson, children may fail the Piaget tests not because they lack the ability to de-centre but because they do it too readily. Here's an example from her beautifully argued essay, *Children's Minds*:

Take two sticks of equal length and show the children that, when lined up, the sticks correspond at each end … Piaget then showed that if you say 'watch this' and push the top stick slightly to the right, then ask children about the length of the sticks, they will suggest that the one just moved is now longer.

Piaget's conclusion was that children fail to appreciate that an object – the stick – will conserve its length and other properties through time because they are incapable of reasoning from a de-centred perspective. In fact, as Donaldson goes on to argue, it is far more likely that they are watching what the adult does – pushing one stick to one side – and assuming that the question is related to the adult's actions. 'Ah, she moved that one, now she's asking me about the same one, she must intend the question to relate to the change she's just made.' In other words, the children are placing greater emphasis on what they take to be adult intentions than on the words of the question; they are attempting to de-centre, to mind-read. It is Piaget who failed to de-centre because he didn't imagine what children would make of his question. According to Donaldson, Piaget was the victim of his own precise but unnatural logic. Our more unschooled instinct to mind-read, to de-centre, to mentalise, call it what you will, is the tool of choice when it comes to understanding others.

But not for Joe. When we arrive at the school, according to the rules of Joe's mind-blind world the routine continues, as it must, for want of any other guide. Abba's 'Dancing Queen' is cut off mid-jive. In this last act of the journey, familiar scenes uncoil, tense and irresistible. As I fish bags from the car parked in the road outside the school, gathering thoughts cling to every move. We let ourselves through the gates into the drive, Joe running ahead to ring the bell, habit getting the better of foreboding, and then stepping back a pace or two to watch the tall Victorian door swing open. The welcome is always cheerful.

'Hello, Joe!'

'A good weekend?'

'How are you Joe?'

We enter to a chorus of encouragement, climbing the steps as Joe peers ahead to see who greets us. Inside the brightly lit hallway there's a small bustle of staff, all smiles. Joe sits obediently to have his shoes removed, stretching out each leg in turn. As soon as they're off, before I've put them in their cubby hole by the door, he scuttles away for the next scene, which takes place on a large shapeless sofa by the window in the playroom, where, as I follow, he pats a space beside him for me to sit down, climbs on top of me and flops into a sad, languid, hug.

He remembers something. Looking round, he finds my hands and leads them around his waist so that I'm holding him. If they stray, he brings them back. We sit like this for perhaps twenty minutes. Sometimes as I chat with his carers about how he's getting on, he lifts his head, examines my lips and eyes, trying hard to see if these are the words that signal departure, and then, when I stay seated, he slumps into me again. Sometimes he rouses himself and we look at a book or sing a song, before he remembers why we're here and puts my hands back in place. The minutes pass. Dinner time isn't far away. After a while, I say:

'OK, Joe, time for me to go now. You be a good boy. Sleeps first and then Mummy and Daddy again.'

He recognises his cue. Unhappy, quiet and with such open-mouthed vulnerability that I forget every testing moment, but still purposeful even in sadness, he dashes ahead, into the hall and rattles up the stairs without looking back. His carer manages a quick goodbye and we smile knowingly, then she skips after him. Joe is already galumphing to the playroom on the first floor which looks to the front of the house.

I key in the door code and let myself out, walk down the drive, through the always-to-be-closed-after-you iron gates with the 5 mph sign. On the pavement, where the view to the window is clearer, I turn and look up through the trees, under the street-lamp. Silhouetted against the light on the first floor is a small boy I know to be Joe, standing on the cushions in the window seat as only he stands, one arm raised above his head, resting against the pane, a tilted look, from the side of his eyes, quite still.

I wave. I say, 'Bye, Joe.' He doesn't move, though he'll be saying 'Bye' quietly. His carer standing nearby waves to encourage him. Joe stands and looks. He'll peer after the car until it disappears from view; he always does. I wave a little longer. Joe, in silhouette, gazes, cheek pressed to the glass. I turn and climb into the car. One more wave. Haunted by his silhouette, I drive into the street-lit winter afternoon. As the car starts, so does the tape. I decide that Abba is pop genius after all, and turn it off.

# 6
# Self-consciousness

Avon Country Park is not slick; the signs are more likely to be painted plywood than neon. To find it, you turn from the A4 Bath road over a humpback bridge, pass the municipal rubbish dump and jolt through potholes alongside fields of cabbages and sweetcorn.

But it is charming. Up from the banks of the coiled river where the ducks shuffle and sit, shuffle and sit, past the flapping tents and hay bales, the miniature railway, the tractor and rusting trailer offering rides, not far from the burgers and peas, you amble from the car park through this patchwork of modest ambition to the top of a gentle hill and the one proud new building.

It was to this oddly pristine industrial barn that I brought Joe shortly after he'd started school, at the end of a day out. He'd already played on the fraying, bouncy slides, then on the long silver slides outside; he'd climbed a bit, he'd lathered himself in ice creams, and of what he'd done he'd tired. There was one place left to try to keep him entertained.

We stepped inside and the doors opened on a cacophony of children, the steel rafters surely ringing, loud enough ordinarily to terrify Joe, whose apprehension held him back, until, that is, he clocked another slide.

Joe likes slides, and here he met the divine archetype of all he'd ever seen: fifty metres of swift, undulating colour, four tracks in a row. We flipped off his shoes, collected a sack to sit in, clambered up the metal stairs, positioned sack on slide, sat down … nearly. Then stood up. Joe retreated. He didn't want to go. He'd changed his mind and pulled me away towards the stairs. Not too steep, but perhaps too long or too fast, the slide had abruptly lost its appeal.

At the bottom, he watched the children whooping down and changed his mind again; we returned to the top.

And then to the bottom, running against the herd. I didn't mind at first, thinking Joe was drumming up courage. Yes, no, yes, no; desire competing with fear, the idea tussling with his senses. Sometimes we'd get a little closer to launching ourselves before his resistance flared and he scrambled away. Each time his reaction was categorical: no, emphatically no; half a minute later, yes, insistently, yes.

I had a hunch he'd like it, but didn't want to force him, so we persisted, another ten minutes, up and down, and then another, less tolerant, until, with all encouragement failing, something in me snapped and I spun from patience to irritation:

'Joe! Up and down, up and down. Will you make up your mind?'

'Sss,' he says. Yes.

So we head to the top.

'Naghh,' he says.

And we thread our way back to the bottom.

'Ssss.'

'Joe!' I look him square in the face and try to keep the lid on something Neanderthal. 'If we go up and down those bloody steps. One. More. Time ...'

'Ssss.'

'Right. Last chance.'

And I stomped him to the top where he wriggled and wrestled, plonked in front of me, held tight and clawing; but too late now, we hurtled forward. It was fast all right, airborne in places, and we rasped to a halt on matting at the end.

'Genn!' he shouted, with a rapturous look.

'Genn!' the word losing itself in excited squeak.

So I spent the next hour feeding Joe's exuberance as he squealed and flapped through slide after gleeful slide, charging up stairs and flying down until the time came to leave and I could scarcely prise him away.

All of us feel indecision, unsure of our desires; few can dither quite like Joe, who'd have vacillated all day, and can be resolute in one contradictory desire hard on the next. Much as he loves swimming, demands it every day, even incessantly, there are occasions he'll pester all morning and, when the time comes, refuse to go. We set off regardless and he's in rebellion every step, into the car, across the car park, past reception, then with the first sight of water, transformed: happy, revelling, and finally refusing to leave, seeming to forget every ounce of earlier antithetical resistance.

Games adored and obsessed over take a handbrake-turn and

are shouted down, as if he forgets the pleasure he took in them. Such a pickle of impulses is he on occasion that you might say, with the trivial use of a pregnant phrase, that he doesn't know, or seems to forget, his own mind. There may be more truth in this than we realise.

Like the face of a Picasso, Joe shows us many aspects at once. One is the Joe who seems to conceive people as functionaries, machines essentially, or at least often treats them as such, suggesting no sense of their inner consciousness. Another is the Joe cleaving to me in frightened need, whose unblinking, open-mouthed, agitated stare meets mine in heartfelt, human vulnerability, who seizes my hands and wraps them about him.

'Oh dear,' he might say with quiet, sing-song understatement, when one of us leaves him.

'Oh dear,' pronounced more clearly than any other phrase he knows.

'Oh dear,' several times over.

Is this Joe reaching between the bars of the cell? When he is sad, and trying to express it, are we justified in counting him evidence of one human grasping for another? If so, how can these moments be consistent with Joe's human isolation, his mind-blindness?

It feels as though I rap his grasping fingers to say so, but his emotions might arise without any sense of my humanity, as we see all too easily by imagining the fondness people feel for inanimate things: some for their car, others for the sofa, their books, a guitar, ornaments or their tweezers. Joe's feelings for me, given extra twist by his compulsiveness, might be no more than this.

Is that fair to him, to debase his anxiety like this? I honestly don't know; I fear it often might be, so that his attachment to me is in consequence of my unique degree of convenience: 'What a useful accessory my Dee is; how lost I am without it.' This is certainly possible, but also deeply uncertain, and not knowing beckons me towards insanity. Nor need the answer, whichever way it falls, be absolute; there might be degrees of understanding, occasional glimmers of recognition in Joe that I have an inner life and feelings for him which, once recognised, he urgently wants to touch and hold. They might equally be glimmers in a prevailing darkness. That much I do believe is possible, but little more.

And the riddle deepens: hard as it is to know what Joe thinks about other people who are close to him, it's harder still to know what, if anything, he thinks about himself.

This is unsettling territory. Self-consciousness, for that's what we're dealing with here, is one of the triumphant distinctions of human kind, and there are reasons – terrible, unhinging reasons – for wondering how much, if any, Joe has, whether his difficulty knowing his own mind on slides and elsewhere is in part because he's not well acquainted with it.

The first reason for doubt is the strong association between self-consciousness and the remarkable capacity for folk psychology that was the subject of the last chapter. These skills seem in some cases related, suggesting that lack of one might imply lack of the other. Indeed, Nicholas Humphrey argues that the two are tightly bound together, and that self-consciousness exists only because it helps us to mind-read.

'My thesis,' says Humphrey, 'is that Nature's solution to the problem of doing psychology has been to give to every member of the human species both the power and the inclination to use a privileged picture of his own self as a model for what it is like to be another person.'

In other words, Humphrey suggests, knowing what others are thinking came with an inseparable companion in being better aware of what we ourselves are thinking, that is, in self-aware-ness. The key to mind-reading is introspection, for therein lies a model of consciousness that we take to be universal. But Hum-phrey goes further, suggesting that such self-awareness arose precisely because of the advantage it gave us in knowing what others are up to. It's a bold argument, that thoughts about our own thoughts – the glorious pinnacle of human sophistication – are simply a by-product. If he is right, that learning to guess what goes on in others' heads equips us with a faculty to exam-ine the meanderings in our own, then the conclusion is inescap-able: the value of everyday mind-reading, says Humphrey, lies in the fact that it is the precursor to self-consciousness itself.

You might want to insist that causality was the other way round: self-consciousness came first, was selected for other reasons, and thus made empathy accidentally possible. You might want to insist that self-consciousness was a divine spark and not an evolutionary adaptation at all, a spark subsequently enabling us to relate with sophistication to other humans. Most Darwinians would say it was a mistake to see self-consciousness as the strategy of nature to do anything with purpose; that that's not how nature works. Self-consciousness, they'd say, was a mutation, a fluke, with all manner of favourable consequences. None of these differences is critical here; whatever the chain of causality that brought self-consciousness about, the argument remains powerfully suggestive: that self-understanding and social understanding have a remarkable intimacy; the way we perceive others is the mirror image of the way we interrogate ourselves.

Were it true that the mirror image – one self-consciousness reflecting another – couldn't be relied on, that your beetle, to use Wittgenstein's analogy, differed significantly from mine, I would have trouble describing my motivations and passions in terms that made sense to you. But I don't. I say 'love' and you know what I mean; your beetle has been there, I see, even if by a different route. Humphrey says we seem to have no practical difficulties communicating these feelings:

> The fact is that, whatever may be the logical problems of describing inner experience, human beings everywhere attempt it ... Indeed, far from being something which baffles human understanding, the open discussion of one's inner experience is literally child's play to a human being, something which children begin to learn before they are more than two or three years old. And the fact that this common sense vocabulary is acquired so easily suggests that this form of description is natural to human beings precisely because it maps directly

onto an inner reality which each individual, of himself, innately knows.

This is known as the argument from analogy and, as philosophers point out, it is utterly unverifiable. As we're beginning to see, that doesn't seem to stop us deploying it with abandon.

Most of us, that is, for in Joe's case I have no such easy emotional rapport, child's play or not, and this points to a troubling question: if it's true that mind-reading and introspection go together, that we're capable of the former as a result of the latter, and if it's true that Joe can't do the former, can't mind-read, does it imply that he also lacks the latter, lacks rich self-consciousness?

In an experiment which would be beyond Joe but might tell us something of what he understands, very young children are given a tube of Smarties and asked what's inside. 'Smarties,' they say. The tube is opened and they discover a pencil. They're then asked what they thought was in the tube before they opened it. 'A pencil,' they say. Furthermore, if they are asked what they think another person will say who hasn't yet looked inside, when asked the same question, they now answer 'a pencil'.

Normal children quickly grow out of this, autistic children often don't. Researchers speculate that these results imply limited self-consciousness, since those who answer 'a pencil' seem unable to examine their own former mental states, seem not to be able to reflect that they once thought 'Smarties'. The age at which they become capable of thinking about their prior, mistaken thoughts is the age at which they also realise others can make the same mistake. Can that timing be coincidence? If it's true, as the experimental evidence suggests, that introspection matures in tandem with awareness of other people's minds, it might, once again, hint at interdependence.

But not always; for there's also evidence that self-consciousness can survive in those with mind-blindness. Many people with Asperger's and one or two other more peculiar and extremely rare conditions are keenly aware of their own states of mind yet curiously blinkered to other people's. It seems they can feel the sting of tears and reflect deeply on the misery that pricked them, but yet see another crying and be utterly lacking any instinctive understanding of the emotional state inside. In such people, mind-blindness must have a cause other than impaired self-consciousness.

Through a website for people with Asperger's, I came across a thirty-three-year-old American whose username is Magic. In answer to some prying questions, Magic frankly described his own sense of awareness of others and of himself.

'I am also not used to thinking about thoughts of other people,' he says, 'and find the notion of others' sentience counterintuitive ... At the age of twenty-six I abandoned the theory positing that I was the only sentient being in existence, and accepted the notion that other people had independent minds. I remember thinking how preposterous that notion seemed.'

And does that difficulty correlate with a lack of self-consciousness?

'In my opinion I have a rather well developed introspection, but I must admit that this development happened gradually only in the last ten years. For a couple of years prior to that, I had rather strange theories about myself and others.' He later added in a note to me that these memories now seemed 'speculative', all of which suggests to me that lack of self-consciousness and lack of awareness of others can indeed run together.

Perhaps Joe will develop as Magic has, but for the time being this doubt about Joe's capacity for one of the core attributes of humanity rattles me to the bones. I cannot write about it without seeing again his blue-grey eyes looking into mine with a gaze that seems to scour my soul. And yet I've wondered if he isn't just bewitched by the reflecting light, perhaps the light of his own image on their surface, so that even what appears deep is shallow. Is he self-conscious or not? If he has some self-consciousness, how much?

What makes me shrink from any conclusion is a suggestion by the philosopher Galen Strawson:

Maybe we are in some deep and inalterable way incapable of really being able to believe that someone whose external behaviour is like Joe's has an emotional life that is in at least some fundamental respects like our own (simply because we don't get the signals we are innately tuned to expect). Maybe we are as incapable of truly believing this about a severely autistic person as a severely autistic person is of grasping that other people have emotional lives (or at least inner lives) that are in fundamental respects like his or her own. This may seem implausible at first, but on reflection I don't see why we should be more surprised one way than the other.

I'm moved by this, the possibility that the failure is ours. In the end, we cannot know how deep is Joe's self-consciousness, though that doubt offers both hope and disquiet. It means we might already have the faculties to enable us one day to connect, Joe and I, but it might also deepen the pity of our current disconnection; for if we do have a similar self-consciousness, we have so far been unable to prove it or share it. How sad that we communicate so badly that we cannot establish even this about one another, cannot hear any echo of ourselves in each other, and so presume, perhaps wrongly, that there is none.

Partly because of this ambiguity, I'm not sure where I would rather the answer lay for Joe: self-conscious, or not? My doubt is compounded by what sometimes happens to some people with Asperger's: their intense self-awareness informs them that there's something about life that they just don't get, and they can experience an agonising, knowing desire for normality without ever quite grasping what normality is. Not all suffer thus, it is true; some remain content, even militantly content with their detachment. Some come to terms with it, develop strategies to cope, yearn to overcome it, but remain puzzled. Magic tells me it caused him deep depression for two years and it's unquestionably true that to be aware of the difference can exact a price. Perhaps in some cases it is better to remain unaware. That's a conclusion I resist, however, being generally of the view that knowledge is better than ignorance, but I shudder at what Joe would make of it, the extent to which he is different, were he capable of making anything of it at all. As I have watched Joe and pitched between various unsatisfactory answers to the question of his self-consciousness, it became the one problem more than any other over which I used to hang my head in perplexed defeat, though not now in despair.

The reason is that not so very long ago Joe started to do something he'd never done before but has since done often. Sitting in the red armchair with the sprung back, which he so loves to fling himself against and come recoiling upright, over and over again, he stopped and cackled wickedly, then boomed:

'Go!'

'Go' is his word for Joe, since he is unable to pronounce the J.

'Go! Pee!'

'Peeeee!'

And he stretched his lips and pointed to his teeth to show a smile, lingering over the long vowel as if posing for a photograph. He knew, and he wanted to tell me, and though I could dismiss this self-knowledge as primitive in scope, even find a reductive explanation for it, I have no desire to. 'Pee' from Joe means happy.

# 7
# Storytelling

There are no pirates in Joe's school, no cops and robbers, cowboys and Indians. Mostly boys, aged in his house between about nine and thirteen, they are in this way singularly unlike boys. Strange to see, these healthy and in Joe's case robust little imps forgoing the rough-and-tumble role play of their normal ways of association, the slings and arrows typical of boys being boys.

Oh, they play, all right. They bounce about, love being caught, thrown around or tickled, have their toys, their favourite things, swim, slide, swing, sing and shout, have more of that youthful quality of boiling, lidless exuberance than most, and the greatest effort goes into calming them. It's simply an eerie absence of one type of play in particular: imaginative or fantasy play. They do not pretend, Joe's crew, neither by creating their own worlds in which to act, nor by miniaturising scenes from life in toy people or animals. What's missing, what makes this admirable place slightly surreal, is lack of the unreal.

The unreal is a place to which many children with autism seemingly can't go, apparently held back by an odd literalness of imagination. How peculiar that in forsaking fantasy for reality, they become strange. And that is not the only paradox: this inability to explore life through fantasy seems to be associated in them with confusion about how to behave in reality.

One spring morning a few years back I took Joe to our local Do It All DIY store. Joe is … let's say, opinionated … about the places he'll visit, but used to tolerate Do It All because once through the paints and the flat-pack furniture, past pets that are other children's compensation for shopping, but boring and un-alive to Joe, away from the bathroom and kitchen displays, there is a gardening section. Its appeal lies not as one might hope in the scent of spring over the north London suburbs from the living, shivering walls of shrubs and potted plants with flimsy petals; what he loves are the garden sheds and summer houses. He scampers out to that row of creosote-brown boxes, their backs to the perimeter fence, skipping from one to the next, letting himself in, closing the door, clomping on the wooden floor, peering out through the window if there is one, opening the door, running to the next, playing Goldilocks, if only he knew who Goldilocks was.

I needed, I forget now, a screwdriver I think, and led him along the aisle where they hang from their hooks like bats. His hand freed as I reached up, Joe took off. No problem, he always goes the same way, being a creature of a permafrost habit, and in the two seconds it takes me to find the one I want I'll be on his tail and soon snaffle him up on the way to the garden sheds.

But as I turn, reach the end of the aisle and look right towards the sliding doors of the gardening section, Joe isn't there. Never is the sense of absence so visceral as when your child disappears. My heart misfires under a sudden, suffocating dread. He couldn't be that fast. Could he? He *couldn't* be that fast. I'm on my toes to run, somewhere, everywhere, to shout, I look down the aisles ahead of me and see nothing but the bustle of strangers, I look left and … there he is.

There he is, sitting happily among the churning crowds of Saturday-morning shoppers. Sitting, with trousers and under-pants around his ankles, feet swinging. Sitting, on one of the shop-display toilets.

'Please God,' I think, in the way that first thoughts in shock often misbehave, 'let it not be on CCTV.'

Joe is wearing a smile of seraphic serenity; I'm not quite so placid. I picture the grainy images, the zoom picking out the crime in commission, the high-angle proof, time-code in the corner. Scenes from *CrimeWatch* ticking through my imagina-tion, I wonder if there's any way out of this before I'm fin-gered as the delinquent parent of the cheerfully widdling boy, plainly no longer toddler enough to be excused this indignity. I know, I'll gesture to Joe from a safe distance, under cover of the special-offer pine shelving: 'Pssst, rendezvous in the sheds, sunshine, the summer house, third from the left.'

Our escape plotted, I sigh and walk over to him to pull up his clothes. He's giggling, delighted with himself, the object of raised eyebrows but not a word from the crowds of passers-by, stuck I imagine somewhere between disgust and discretion. Standing Joe up, he leans on me and I glance over his shoulder to assess the damage, finding myself thankful it isn't worse than the shallow yellow puddle I see sitting so oddly undiluted in that pit of enamel, wondering where to go. Thankful.

At the time it feels mortifying, but here's the real problem: how do I explain to Joe where he went wrong? It's not real, Joe – that is, it's real but it doesn't work – that is, it does work, but it's not … plumbed in. Hopeless; complexity crowds in from the moment I begin. I say none of this, of course; at the time, all I can think of is: 'Not in shop, Joe; not in shop.' Don't do it in Do It All. But not even that is accurate, I realise, as we pass the designated, plumbed-in facilities on the way out, though even the reality of the genuine article is rendered equivocal by an 'out of order' sign on the door. For Joe, the idea that this or any other toilet could be in any sense unreal would be absurd. Unreality, even qualified reality, probably has little reality for him: looks like a toilet, feels like a toilet, therefore is a toilet.

Joe's problems were once thought to be a result of Hartnup disease, named after an Irish immigrant family in London in the 1960s who, the story goes, used to piss in the back garden with such acidity that it left circles of scorched brown grass. It's relatively easy to diagnose, you could probably get halfway there with a piece of litmus paper in the urine. Coincidentally, Joe's first wet nappies evacuated the house. I wanted a toxic-hazard sign, the kind seen on the side of tankers telling the fire brigade what to squirt on the stuff inside, while the police throw a cordon around to keep passers-by at bay.

Over-anxious, pushy-middle-class, think-they-know-it-all, for-God's-sake-relax parents; this, we felt, was our allotted category in life when in the early days we used to say that something about Joe didn't seem right, and few agreed. Or else, if he wasn't developing normally, it was because compared with his sister he wasn't receiving enough attention, his father didn't read to him as much, what do you expect? So I read to him, and he wrestled out of my lap every time, upset and uninterested. It's extraordinary, this instinct to blame the parents, and most notorious in the case of Bruno Bettelheim who coined that perniciously influential notion of the 'refrigerator mother' to explain the emotional withdrawal seen in children with autism. What was wrong with these children, Bettelheim believed, was that their cold-fish mothers didn't cuddle them enough. When I told some of Joe's stories in a short series on Radio 4, one listener wrote to say that if only the four family members would sit down and admit their mistakes then Joe would get better.

Recognition that there was a developmental problem, any problem, took nearly two years in Joe's case. Giving it a name, Hartnup, an irrelevant name in my view, took nearly another. In Hartnup, the urine is acidic because it contains higher than normal levels of amino acids which the body is adept both at keeping out and getting rid of. This strange reaction to proteins was the only potential culprit we could find for Joe's disability, with the level of two amino acids in particular giving concern: threonine and tryptophan. The diagnosis suggested an obvious chemical remedy: if there wasn't enough of the stuff in there, put in some more. It wasn't so easy, the body's defences being every bit as good at filtering it out before it found its way to where it was thought to be needed, in the cerebro-spinal fluid. Researchers in California had suggested that by bolting these amino acids onto alcohol molecules to create tryptophan ethyl ester and threonine methyl ester, the alcohol would smuggle the proteins through his digestive wall and across the blood/brain barrier, falling away as they did so: drop some hooch the way of the body's overactive border defences to confuse them and the immigrant proteins would escape to enrich the chemical stew on the other side, in his brain. We tracked down a source of these adapted proteins and applied the theory for several years, hoping to detect a practical difference. I don't think it made any. To the consultant's credit, she never thought it would.

Based in Crewe, CLIMB (Children Living with Inherited Metabolic Diseases – previously the Research Trust for Metabolic Diseases in Children) campaigns and fundraises for research into metabolic disorders, of which there are some 1,300. It also puts parents of those affected in touch with one another. Hearing that Joe had a variety of Hartnup with neurological symptoms, they told us it affected perhaps half a dozen people in Britain and gave us details of two other families: one in Ireland, one in Australia. Neither case bore much resemblance.

In Do It All some four or five years on, that long saga of blaming the parents, doubt that there was a problem at all, and the many wrong turns we all took would have felt unreal and irrelevant, a whole dockside of red herrings. Given time, the fact of Joe's problem became glaringly obvious, though even at seven one consultant was calling him 'not at all autistic' while another called him 'a classic case'. One reason it takes so long to be sure is that autism has no aetiology, no assigned cause, and it is through unusual social behaviour that Joe's condition most conspicuously declares itself, which means that diagnosis is easiest when he most blatantly breaks social rules, rules which don't take proper shape until children are generally well into nursery age or later. Biology has proved useless, so far.

The social rules, from the point of view of an autistic child, are a thicket of all-too-subtle traps and pitfalls. I beat out my brains trying to think how to simplify these rules for Joe and, later in the day of the Do-It-All débâcle, experience a short-lived rapture – such is the stuff that passes for enlightenment when stuck in this mental rut – that weeing is best explained as something you don't do in front of other people, until men's urinals spring to mind. With that failure, I reflect that I'm not quite sure in any case how to explain to Joe within the scope of the language he understands the idea of absence, as in the absence of other people, for it requires the absent thing to be invoked, to be present in the imagination before we instantly show it the exit and admit that it is not present really, not physically, the very playfulness with the unreal that Joe finds so difficult. All this is neatly expressed from a young age by the rest of us in a simple phrase such as, 'not with other people about'. Those few short words suddenly stun me with their complexity. I realise I'm incapable of unpicking their meaning into component ideas or stating their essence in a way Joe could understand, and the thought takes a cattle prod to familiarity, so wrecking the whole project of simplification. Then, catching myself ruminating on the ontology of British attitudes to urinating, I'm a mess of laughter.

Composed again and wondering if toilet etiquette isn't after all the apotheosis of the human condition, I reflect on what makes the rules so complicated and why the rest of us learn them with such fluency. I see that in the absence of the normal child's precocious absorption of social norms, I'd need to explain explicitly and in detail to Joe a bewildering variety of elaborate concepts – privacy, embarrassment, hygiene – a quick word like 'dirty' used as a moral metaphor, the sort of tool we typically use, just wouldn't do. I instantly see the dismal fact that I haven't a prayer.

How do the rest of us manage? One answer is with the help of those now familiar sidekicks, mind-reading and its near relative, acute self-consciousness. Only humans blush, and for that remarkable reason: our presumption to know, without them telling, what others think of us. So called first-order emotions include happiness, anger, fear and surprise and are expressed easily by autistic children, though sometimes in surprising contexts. Privacy and embarrassment depend on the second-order emotions of guilt and shame, which rely on a richer self-consciousness, a sense of how we appear to others, which Joe hardly seems to express at all.

Our other advantage, the critical and related one at issue here, is that we, unlike Joe and his schoolmates, have a strong capacity for the unreal. This makes the idea of a display toilet more easily comprehensible to us, but it does much more than that. One example from a real case hints at the distinction: an autistic adult with above average IQ was told that the drinks were on the house. He understood this to mean that if he wanted a drink then 'on the house' was where he'd have to go. He was, as one writer put it, unable to escape from the salience of reality.

The unreal has many forms of which pretence, irony, metaphor and imagination are just a few. Between them, these gifts unlock immense possibilities of meaning and understanding, and nowhere more so than in relation to the normal traffic of our social world. Important as any among them when it comes to learning correct behaviour, I believe, is storytelling.

In his autobiography and memoir of reading, Francis Spufford writes of the power of the words that came foaming through the fiction of his childhood:

> They help form the questions we think are worth asking; they shift around the boundaries of the sayable inside us, and the related borders of what's acceptable; their potent images, calling on more in us than the responses we will ourselves to have, dart new bridges into being between our conscious and unconscious minds, between what we know we know, and the knowledge we cannot examine by thinking. They build and stretch and build again the chambers of our imagination.

If Spufford is right about the developmental benefits of the unreal, one can quickly speculate about the effect on Joe, who in common with most autistic children has little sense for narrative, seems uncertain about the borders of the fictional, and performs almost no socio-dramatic play. Could it be that the difficulty he has negotiating social occasions, in Do it All and elsewhere, is a direct consequence? Are the chambers of his imagination unbuilt, unstretched, his boundaries of the acceptable unformed in part because stories make no sense to him?

Spufford titles his opening chapter 'Confessions of an English Fiction Eater'. He reads fiction with a hunger for anything absent at the time of reading; any greedy wish will do, he says. For what fiction does is to give breath to what is not. It allows us to explore other possibilities, see them made fictional flesh, work out the consequences of transgression, to inhabit ideas. Moreover, we do so in a controlled environment where no one is really hurt, no monster loosed, no heart broken, no tragedy sprung, no one punished, but where we can sample our feelings in such cases, play with them, give them exercise, become better acquainted with them. We need a place where the human spirit can experiment, among the test tubes in laboratories of mad professors, the fierce emotions of star-crossed lovers, children trapped on desert islands. Fiction, in this account, is a variety of educational play or pretence. Stories focus emotions for us, as Spufford says; we enfold ourselves into them, and in that embrace we learn about the emotions and ourselves. Here is a great playground of the unreal where Joe seemingly cannot go, an exploration of social experience that Joe can never undertake.

In Oliver Sacks' account of his meeting with the autistic Temple Grandin he writes: 'She was bewildered, she said, by

*Romeo and Juliet* ("I never knew what they were up to") and with *Hamlet* she got lost with the back and forth of the play. Though she ascribed these problems to "sequencing difficulties," they seemed to arise from her failure to empathise with the characters, to follow the intricate play of motive and intention. She said that she could understand "simple, strong, universal" emotions but was stumped by more complex emotions and the games people play.'

Causality in storytelling often depends on states of mind: she *loved* him, he *loved* her, but *falsely believing* her dead all ended in disaster. Grandin's problem is the stitching between events, the psychological and emotional states that supply motivation. Narrative is a means of giving order to the world, but without this emotional stitching narrative instantly loses all coherence as human actions are left bereft of causation. There's experimental evidence that if autistic children who enjoy reading are given books with blank spaces between words, often they seem unable to guess what's missing. If silly words are substituted here or there, they often don't seem to mind, even though this makes a nonsense of the global sense of the story. Unpick the causal, psychological stitching and they're unfazed because they probably weren't paying it much heed in the first place; their enjoyment of books must be based on something other than narrative logic.

When we observe Joe's consumption of stories, what do we see? He reads books as if they are not stories at all, but rather a series of snapshots, one page in proximity to the next, maybe, but not necessarily related. Watching him watch videos, I have the feeling he absorbs them scene by isolated scene, not with continuity. Like Temple Grandin, he probably feels mystified by motivation and intention, by Pat's reasons for stopping on his round to have a cup of tea, a cake and a chat with Granny Dryden. 'Teat,' – (something) to eat – says Joe, observing the fact but not really knowing why it occurred. The result must be that much of life doesn't flow one thing to another so much as arrive in lumps in his lap. Not being able to see the psychological connections between events means that even if I gave Joe a telling off, he might often be unsure why; moreover, I'm honestly not sure what Joe thinks Postman Pat is: a copy of reality, a representation of it, or a reality in itself?

My friend Katey tells me of her niece, Rose, who wanted to play a game: 'Let's pretend Mummy and Daddy are dead and we have to go and live in an orphanage,' she says. When I argue that socio-dramatic play helps us understand social events, I'm not suggesting that Rose is educating herself to cope specifically in the event of her parents' early and no doubt gruesome death. Stories are not literal rehearsals, they have more generic power than that; they probably serve as archetypes for many experiences, in this case perhaps the many forms of separation she might experience in life.

Christopher Booker's recent work, *The Seven Basic Plots*, is an encyclopaedic feat of categorisation, arguing in common with some others that stories are displaced myths. He rounds them up under titles like 'Voyage and Return' or 'Overcoming the Monster' and it seems, he says, that they work as archetypes because of some deep resonance in the unconscious, in the way our psyche organises experience, perhaps, according to one reviewer of Booker's work, because narrative patterns, experienced from childhood, have priority over conscious thought; that is, when we wonder how to explain what's going on around us, our first instinct is to reach for an archetypal story, rather than to sit back in analytical contemplation. Speaking for my own trade, that certainly seems to be the way journalism works, defining events in terms of commonplace narratives such as 'the betrayal', 'the feud', 'the pledge', 'the bungle'. Though we're all taught to avoid clichés, the fact seems to be that newspapers in particular (and perhaps readers) are happier once a story can be nailed down in terms of one or another stock theme.

In creating fictions during play, are we not learning about and establishing in our developing minds the same kind of myths? Susan Isaacs, a psychologist, writes that 'play is indeed the child's work, and the means whereby he grows and develops. Active play can be looked upon as a sign of mental health; and its absence ... of mental illness.' There's some support for the idea that pretend play is social education from another study, by Wendy Haight and Peggy Miller in 1993, which found that three-quarters of pretend play is social, not solitary. In 1987, Alan Leslie, a former research associate of Uta Frith, wrote a paper suggesting that an important capacity of the human mind was the ability to decouple representation from reality:

The perceiving, thinking organism ought, as far as possible, to get things right. Yet pretence flies in the face of this fundamental principle. In pretence we deliberately distort reality. How odd then that this ability is not the sober culmination of intellectual development but instead makes its appearance playfully and precociously at the very beginning of childhood ... how is it possible for a child to think about a banana as if it were a telephone, a lump of plastic as if it were alive or an empty soap dish as if it contained soap?

Once you can form a mental representation unshackled from reality, you can play with it, imagine it otherwise, project it onto others as a way of accounting for what they do, use it to help organise experience. We can, as in Francis Spufford's description of the value of fiction, build and stretch and build again the chambers of our imagination. Without that skill, without an ability to bring to life what is not, or what might be, or to take what has been and arrange it in patterns with which we feel comfortable, we have only a chaotic hailstorm of what is, and only what is on the surface at that. We cannot hypothesise, speculate or – and here the deficit is alarming but has to be faced – imagine.

I do not know how deep this deficit goes in Joe; he simply must be able to invoke an image or idea, of pasta, say, in order to ask for it when it isn't there. I suspect, though, that it is an inflexible image, not one he would consider playing with in the imagination, and perhaps this inflexibility accounts for his own love of routine; perhaps another of the ways in which we are able to cope with variation, flux and change is because the imagination has accustomed us to such alteration, it has previewed so many changes that we become comfortable with the process of change. With every degree that Joe's thoughts have to move into what is not here, not now and not him, he seems to find increasing difficulty. The rest of us are masters at imagining and manipulating the world, near or far, in our thoughts, and we do it relentlessly. It is another commonplace for us, a skill we take for granted, but a sign of extravagant mental dexterity.

Sometimes Joe will bring into jumbling collision a plastic Postman Pat in his left hand and a Mrs Goggins in his right as if in some unlikely lecherous congress on the post office counter, but I'm not sure what's actually going on, whether Joe is acting out a scene or simply crashing plastic. Even if the former, the scope of behaviours he plays out must be tiny, for it usually involves his plastic figures gliding through the space in front of him as he sits in an armchair. Pat the astronaut? I don't think so. In general, it is striking, this lack of feeling for the pretend among autistic children. They do not engage in ordinary spontaneous symbolic play with dolls, nor in role play. Sometimes when prompted by example, Joe will offer Pat a bite of biscuit, but never on his own initiative.

Thus the educating capacity of the stories that are told to us, or the pretend games we play, whether as proxies for experience or places to flex the imagination and work out what's sayable and acceptable, are probably largely lost on Joe.

Can we be sure the ability to decouple reality and representation is linked to social competence? When Joe decides to take off his clothes in the café because he's spilt a lone drip on his T-shirt, when he hits babies or grabs strangers' food from their plates if it takes his fancy, it's unquestionably true that he mistakes the boundaries of the acceptable. Had he been able to explore the unreal, would it have helped him? Up to a point, I think it might.

Normal infants learn specifics about the world, direct facts, says Uta Frith, but by the second year, they go a step further and show the first signs of learning to form representations of what other people think about those facts. The difference is profound, beginning as it does to make possible the development of children's ideas about not just an object itself but anything that another person might hold in her head about it. Paul Harris, a developmental psychologist, has written that we use an 'as if' mechanism to think ourselves into someone else's predicament. Thus can Mummy pick up a banana and pretend it is the telephone and the child instantly cotton on to what she's doing, instantly see that she is holding in her head an attitude to the banana that is not dictated by the fact of it being a banana. Seeing me speak into a banana, Joe would write it off as another of the mysterious ways of people, with no apparent sense or purpose.

This helps us see why pretence of this kind might be linked to social understanding. Pretence is a mental attitude. Social acceptability is likewise determined by mental attitudes: if I use a banana like a telephone, it is only like a telephone because of my attitude towards it. If I take care to wear clothes in public it is partly because I am aware of the mental attitudes of those who might disapprove if I was naked. Therefore, if I can understand pretence, I am also more likely to be capable of understanding that other people can have diverse mental attitudes towards the people and things around them, similar skills being deployed in both cases. Possessed of that understanding, I might even become mindful of those attitudes and try to make sure my behaviour doesn't offend them. So it seems perfectly plausible that we use the same piece of mental machinery for understanding others as we do for exploring the unreal.

Alan Leslie, who first suggested this line of thought, proposed that in most of us the developmental origins of our sense that other people have minds lie in the capacity for pretence. His argument is controversial. In support, there is some evidence from small studies that children who do engage in more socio-dramatic play have a better understanding of social situations and particularly of other people's motivations, but the statistical basis for these findings is insufficiently robust. Yet there is this signal piece of uncontested evidence: children with autism, a condition defined principally by deficient social awareness, don't do socio-dramatic play. This strong association does not imply causation, of course, in either direction, but it certainly suggests a link.

A final, bizarre indication of the lack of such a decoupling mechanism in autistic children, one that has obvious repercussions for their social life, is that they find it exceedingly hard to lie or to detect lies. Oliver Sacks says that Temple Grandin was an easy victim of tricks and exploitation who failed 'to understand dissembling and pretence … missed allusions, presuppositions, irony, metaphor, jokes …'.

Most children understand jokes with word-sounds of multiple meaning by about the age of six: 'What's black and white and red all over? A newspaper.' 'Why was 6 afraid of 7? Because 7, 8, 9.' But every child I know has been through some phase, much younger, aged about three or four, where bouncing down the stairs is even funnier to the rhythm of 'wee, wee, poo, poo, bum, bum' that so makes parents smirk at one another. Taking delight in exploring the borders of rudeness is a recognition of the layers of meaning in words and behaviour, a sense that things and actions have many kinds of representation, and here's one thing – wee – objectively uninspiring, with a layer of meaning that grown-ups are comically twitchy about. Children rejoice in trespassing on language, sounding it out, in or out of context, to see what happens; rabbits on Mr MacGregor's vegetable patch, or dipping a toe into embarrassment and finding it tickles. They already know these things are subject to weird social codes and play helps probe and define the limits. The fact that a single word, 'bum', can be a joke, tells them it has at least two registers. Temple Grandin and others with autism find life easier to understand if the rules are simple, clear and explicit. Sadly, social rules thrive on subtlety; their light shines on behaviour through a prism, where it's fractured for endless different occasions. Embarrassment, which, according to Sacks, Grandin never feels, is a complication born of life's multiple registers, many of them attitudinal: how it looks from here, from there, who's watching, what they know, where you are, what time the event happens. Most of us are busily decoupling representation and reality all the time, to enrich meaning, add emotional shades, social mores, jokes, or lies. If it were possible to have a world of facts alone, without such added layers of representation, Joe, Grandin and others with autism would find it more comprehensible; the rest of us would lose an immeasurable range of subtleties, and laugh not nearly so much.

Joe's inability to imagine that others might see his actions in Do It All differently from the plain facts of the situation – needed a wee, found toilet, did one – means that, like Grandin, he can't be embarrassed; he doesn't care what anyone else thinks and can't be taught. In the hardware store, where I do care, I face a dilemma: it would be unconscionable to slink out without telling someone, but think of the explaining. And yet ... the poor member of staff who'll stumble across it if I don't. Oh sod it, I'm going to have to confess, I think, as we walk towards the tills; there can be no slinking out of this one.

And so we slink out. A metre away from the sliding doors, Joe stops and turns. Not now, Joe, not with escape so close. I half expect the long arm of security to appear brandishing a bucket of incriminating evidence. 'Is this yours, sir?' I yearn to be outside, but Joe insists; he often does.

'What is it, sunshine?' I say wearily, and he reaches up, takes hold of my neck and pulls me into an immense embrace. As the doors slide shut behind us, he's tempted to make them open again, which he knows he can do by going back in; he understands basic cause and effect. But I won't let him and he'll never know why, for the cause and effect in my head is non-existent for Joe. Mind-blindness takes another toll as, on the whole, he assumes my thoughts to be identical to his own, as if his thoughts are all the thoughts there are, as if there is but one great universal thought we all share. With his trousers round his ankles, smiling, I suppose he expected me to feel the same relief.

A few weeks later, out and about in St Albans, Joe tugged on my hand as we passed a bathroom display in a shop window. Why not, he must have wondered, consolidating routine, it worked last time? We found somewhere in the station down the road instead.

There is a story I could tell another child, the story I tell you, about how the strange boy did a wee in a funny place and his daddy ran away; and from that you would learn a great deal about the social acceptability of certain kinds of behaviour. Joe would understand only if I could explain the causation almost mechanistically, talking to my son as if we were such rigid physicists that Newton's laws of motion provided the only acceptable vocabulary. It is as if I need to make explicit understandings that usually strike the rest of us instinctively. Theories of child development, quite rightly, don't generally assume that children learn social behaviour by direct analysis and instruction, taking life apart, pulling open its mechanics, contemplating interaction cog by cog. We do that sort of thing when we're older, when the realisation hits us that what we do with contemptuous ease in childhood is actually rather sophisticated, and then some of us become academics. One wouldn't expect that to be a consideration for any ten-year-old. Sadly, though in Joe's case it might help him make sense of the world, the ambition is lunar.

Learning social behaviour is simpler, more osmotic than that, thank God, at least for those who can do it. On the whole, it is argued, the rules governing our social interaction are either biological or insidiously cultural. That is, we grow into social beings according either to the promptings of our genes, without much effort, or as a result of the environmental broth on which we're nurtured, again with only limited conscious reflection. There is no manual, no intellectual deconstruction necessary; what we know is either there from the outset or it seeps in, an accidental agglomeration: a bit of example here, a word of correction there, play whenever possible, certainly not by the kind of painstaking elucidation Joe seems to require.

Storytelling is similarly hybrid, similarly easy, coming to us like milk from a mother's breast, a nurturing commodity naturally prompted. Storytelling comes in infinite forms but often deals in themes that resound like an echo down the centuries, an echo in our bones. 'What,' asks Francis Spufford, 'is the most embedded form of language, for all that it seems devoted to carrying those who hear it outside the moment? What way of speaking deals out situations one after another, is full of concrete particulars and keeps an eye on people's intentions all the time? What packs in cognitive material most richly in a form children are able to attend to? The story.'

It is, he says, an inheritance which may be as genetic as the upright gait of our branch of primates or opposable thumbs. Imagine life without it. Imagine Joe. We're lucky we can.

# 8
# Innocence

Joe was languid but pensive in the play area outside school. It was mid-December and in little more than a week he'd be home for Christmas. He was preoccupied by the thought, not of Christmas, the tinselled festivities of which don't impress, but of home, scene of his greatest indulgence regardless of the season. Next to him stood a young classmate similar in age and size, a boy of comparable ability and disability who sat with Joe, often shared his Lightwriter and was closer than any to being called his friend.

A pitiful shortcoming in Joe's former home life had been his isolation. We created a unique nest for him where few others came, excluding anything that disrupted his fragile calm, and other children – unforgiving, noisy, uncompromising – were classed as disruptions. If he were to learn, we reasoned, we had enough to do to hold his attention. We came in time to doubt that logic, since he learnt one thing at the expense of another: numbers and colours, for example, rather than the ordinary civilising encounters of social life. School might just, we hoped, supply both.

As Joe got used to the school routine and slowly accepted

the technicolour presence of other children often as odd, disruptive and wired as he, the signs were promising. Our modest hope for him was not a life of intimacies, deep, trusting companionship and rapport – Joe may never know these things – it was simply for a shared experience of social life, of everyday encounters that might sow a seed or two of awareness that others existed. Lately, Joe and his classmate had begun to look like a pair.

Standing together in the playground that day, Joe thumped him.

A raised hand, the open side of a clenched fist, a single blow aimed at the body, not an accomplished strike, not the noble art, but delivered with vicious intent.

A pause.

To Joe's astonishment, the boy hit him back. A raised hand, a similarly pathetic flap, hardly what you'd call a flurry of punches.

Another pause.

Joe slugged him again.

It was as if certain gentlemanly rules applied: you have your whack, sir, then I shall have mine. A cup of tea between blows wouldn't have been out of place. It ended not many stately whacks later when one of Joe's went un-returned and, somehow satisfied with that, the two boys resumed their slouch. Joe, the stubborn devil, had had the last word.

And yet, I want to maintain that Joe is one of life's innocents. By innocence, I mean this definition: that he has little self-awareness, the innocence of childhood extended indefinitely, knowing nothing of the evil in the world, nor conscious how he appears to others. He's helped by a sublime indifference to other people's opinions. Unaware of the bad they do and think, he doesn't see his own nakedness, has little sense of his own privacy, no pride or vanity, bears little malice because – I suspect – he scarcely imagines how others could suffer.

Here, though, is the first note of ambiguity, for to be unable to imagine suffering has a barbed consequence; true, it means never intending to cause real hurt (he hits people the way he presses buttons on the video, with no sense of human pain inside), but it also means being unmoved by their pain, as likely callous as virtuous. With this realisation we begin to see how Joe's innocence is capable of cruelty. One lesson of his behaviour is that as far as we associate virtue with ignorance – the Forrest Gump tendency – we fatally misunderstand it.

One Saturday, Joe and I stood waiting in the Harlequin shopping centre in Watford for the lift to the car park. Joe is rattled by lifts; he approaches them like stalking a rabbit, hunched, one foot gingerly ahead of other, an inchworm towards the precipice. Some heights, but not all, send him scrambling through his dizziness for the folds of my coat, hiding his eyes, covering his head, distrusting the floor. When we're driving, he'll throw himself head down into the seat at the approach of a hill he recognises, grabbing anything solid or substantial as if he's about to fall off – the gearstick, me, his sister Cait – and hold on like a cat. It's a peculiar kind of vertigo because he might just as suddenly throw off his fear, sit up and start flapping or shouting 'weee!' – his word for a slide. Then again, he might not react at all if he hasn't come across the hill before. The same physical event thus variously produces alarm, excitement and indifference.

Around us in the Harlequin centre were the typical units of neon-lit, city Lego: WHSmith, Boots, Dixons, like block-paving in primary colours. Since the alternative to the lift is coaxing him up four flights of stairs and escalators, the lift gets the nod and at least he enjoys pushing the buttons – both of them – though still at arm's length. And so we waited while the indicator counted off the floors, and in that moment, from a pram a few steps away, came the first plaintiff drone of a restless toddler.

Crying babies intrigue Joe. If you're lucky, he points and mimics. 'Uh huh, huh, huh,' he says, meaning, obviously enough: 'crying'. But his recognition of tears can't be taken to mean he understands the feelings that prompt them and so, if you're unlucky, he'll do what he first did that day.

Peering towards the pram, turning with a puzzled look from the toddler to me, he shuffled into a better position to see. The baby's mother looked on serenely, smiling as one sweet little one exhibited cute fascination for another.

'Yes, Joe, baby crying,' I said as he glanced over for some kind of reassurance. 'Baby sad.'

'Uh huh, huh, huh!' said Joe.

'I think he's a little bit tired,' said the mother to Joe.

'Uh huh, huh, huh!'

'Yes, Joe, crying.'

These are mostly words he can make sense of, words he's

heard and understood before, but not with the meaning you and I would attach to them, as it soon transpired. Joe took another step forward, peered closely, raised his hand and smashed his fist into the writhing bundle in the pushchair.

For a breathless moment we stood and gawped. All good clichés deserve their day: we froze on the spot, we really were lost for words, for what does etiquette demand following unprovoked toddler atrocity? I was still staring, stupid with shock, when it dawned on me he was about to do it again, and I jumped gawkily to catch his raised arm.

Judging by the even tone and intensity of the cry, Joe hadn't connected well enough with any tender part to do damage. All the same, it was grotesque; profuse apologies and mumbled explanations scarcely made amends. The baby's mother was understanding, to a point, but clearly couldn't take in the brutality: a baby, for heaven's sake. She stood there a little pale and open mouthed and who can blame her, that she came shopping only to witness an act so confounding her deepest instincts to protect the weak and be tender to unhappiness. From a scene of sweetness and apparent compassion sprang thuggery.

Doubtless, Joe did it, but did he do it with malice? Did he know it to be wrong? A court wouldn't find him criminally responsible and the interesting question is what peculiarity in Joe allows us to say that the court would be right.

'Yes, yes, I understand,' she said, taking in what logic there was in my hasty, garbled explanation, but evidently not caring for it. Thank goodness, I think as I look back, Joe didn't do any real harm. The mother knelt in front of the pushchair, stroking and tucking her toddler, still wincing and perhaps sub-consciously shielding him from us. I'll muse over this one later, I thought as we made our still apologetic exit.

'Yes, do take it,' said the mother, keen to see us off. 'No, no damage. Yes, he's all right.' We shuffled into the lift, Joe sloping along beside me silently chewing his thumb.

Does shame smile? On every page of Joe's life there's been another pop-up disaster. With almost all, an odd laughter also rises in me, lurching between waves of something more des-perate and intense, something a little like grief. This absurd vacillation passes behind closed eyes, my head down, my face somewhere between smirk and grimace, convulsive, doleful sniggers mocking my seriousness. Not, I think (I hope), because I relish moments like this, but because, I reason afterwards, seeing them as comedy is the one alternative to despair. For after the panic comes shame pure and simple. What on earth did I say or do to give Joe the idea that the correct response to crying toddlers is to thump them? Nothing, I hope, but truly, who knows? Later, a friend tried to console me with the thought that there are adults among us who also think vio-lence is a proper tool of upbringing, but putting Joe in that class is no comfort.

Joe, on the other hand, gave no indication of guilt or any-thing like it. I'm not sure how he would express guilt, so could be wrong, but surmised from his blithe expression and happy chatter once we were out of the lift and back in the car park that he felt no particular moral questions had been raised.

Compare Joe's behaviour with the story of Yoni, a chimpan-zee raised by Nadie Ladygina Kohts in Moscow in the early twentieth century.

'If I pretend to be crying,' wrote Kohts, 'close my eyes and weep, Yoni immediately stops his play and any other activities, quickly runs over to me, all excited and shagged, from the most remote places in the house, such as the roof or the ceiling of his cage, from where I could not drive him down despite my persistent calls and entreaties. He hastily runs around me, as if looking for the offender; looking at my face, he tenderly takes my chin in his palm, lightly touches my face with his finger, as though trying to understand what is happening and turns around, clenching his toes into firm fists.'

The story is told by the primatologist Frans de Waal in his book *The Ape and the Sushi Master*. It's one among many remarkable examples of animal empathy for both other animals and humans. Chimps do it, most humans first begin to show signs of it from about twenty months, a feeling of empathy. In all likelihood, Joe doesn't feel empathy now, aged ten, and might never.

For most of us, the ability to recognise a set of basic human emotions is near universal. Show pictures of a happy, smiling face or a sad, weeping one, and just about everyone, in every culture, agrees what they mean. The experiment has been tried, the results are overwhelmingly positive. And Joe? Joe I know recognises expressions: he can name a smile, a crying face or an angry one – the first-order emotional expressions – and produce consistent words or sounds approximating to the correct description for each. He can point to a crying face when we say the word 'sad'. But I suspect it's mostly veneer to Joe. It's all on the outside, noise and salt and water, nothing to do with what he knows from his own aching heart or shrieking nerve endings when he also cries.

A friend, finding herself alone with Joe for a moment or two while he shelled a packet of fruit pastilles into his mouth, asked if she could have one, held out her hand and when he ignored her pretended to cry. She might as well have been invisible, she said. It could be that Joe saw through her, though I suspect the truth is in the other direction entirely: that he could barely see her as a rounded psychological being at all, with wants, needs or feelings distinct from his own chomping sense of growing satiety. Here, then, is another likely casualty of Joe's mind-blindness: as with his difficulty in understanding what other people mean when they talk to him, or their motivation when they act around him, so is he unable to work out, with the casual ease so familiar to the rest of us, what they feel.

This is so despite the fact that Joe does cry too, and it is thought to be in large part from familiarity with our own feelings that we suppose others who behave as we do, feel as we do. In making that assumption, as most of us do, we have to be able to imagine a separate mind with separate sensations but working in the same fashion as our own. If we typically found that difficult to imagine, as Joe finds it fiendishly difficult to know what others are feeling, how could we know what would constitute their good? How could we know what virtue was?

For a year or two, Joe went to a school for children with moderate learning difficulties in south Watford. It was an exceptional institution. I was in awe of the devotion of the staff, the head teacher who was wise and helpful, his teachers and carers often loving and dutiful. They laboured to make the placement work and would have battled on gamely with Joe, I suspect, almost whatever happened. It wasn't to be. Joe's behaviour, despite one-to-one support, became steadily more disruptive and violent. In the end they expelled him, not because the school ran out of goodwill, but because we asked them to. Had we withdrawn him voluntarily, we could have been said to have assumed financial responsibility for his education, a ruinous prospect. 'Never been asked to expel a child before,' said the head teacher.

As Joe's behaviour at school deteriorated, the staff kept a log. It made fascinating reading, that by-now golden blend of agony and hilarity that seems to be one of Joe's motifs. When he became difficult, he was taken out of class and left to chill for a couple of minutes in a separate, safe but somewhat spartan room, a kindergarten cooler.

Joe understood this, brilliantly, as an incentive: the way to escape from work was to cause mayhem. The log came home at the end of each day, neatly divided into columns with the time, the nature of the incident and the action taken carefully recorded. 12:23 Joe hit Jimmy. Action taken – two minutes quiet room. 12.26 Joe hit Jimmy. Action taken – two minutes … 12:29 Joe hit …

The problem for the school was what to do with this child

in the confined space of a classroom whenever he turned into the livid flailing squid from *20,000 Leagues Under the Sea* and Jimmy was within range. The answer seemed obvious: take him out of arm's reach, take him where he could do no harm, take him out. Unfortunately, Joe wanted out and the school was unwittingly coaching him to achieve it. He didn't like the bustle, didn't like the more innocent idiosyncrasies of his class-mates, and so, in seeking his own peace, found violence highly effective.

Equally, Joe didn't want to learn. Learning involves novelty whereas he prefers familiarity. Yet the lesson he did master with precocity was that the quickest way to see off all that riled him was an unmeasured right hook. He practised it, to the teach-ers' dismay, with ruthless efficiency, as if pain were not real unless his own. I knew this attitude to my cost when, playing in bed, he'd cantilever his hefty self over my chest on the points of his elbows, sublimely indifferent to the wincing and groan-ing. I used to have a sneaking, perverse regard for the way Joe could reduce responsible, committed adults to rubble, myself among them. Of necessity, I smiled about that in private. Mind you, poor Jimmy.

How do we still call Joe innocent? True, he has no mind of Jimmy, no obvious compassion for his discomfort, just as he had little human regard, it seems, for an 'innocent' baby; but then, he has little mind, little awareness even of himself.

What we sometimes mean by innocence here is what Simon Baron-Cohen describes when he talks of mind-blindness. Mind-blindness, an inability to imagine the state of mind of others, an inability to wonder what they're thinking, is often said to indicate a lack of vanity or pride. Most of us make assumptions about what others know and think all the time. In writing this, I think about how you will think. If you walk towards the corner around which I've just passed a drunken brawl, I know that you will not know about it and I'll probably warn you. Likewise, because I am aware of your thoughts, I might worry about your opinion of me, I might become vain, seek fame, demand respect, shrink in embarrassment. I doubt Joe would have much sense of any of this: being unable to imagine the minds of others, or indeed, I suspect, to imagine in abstract his own thoughts, he lacks both self-awareness and awareness of others to an extent that arguably makes him innocent of his actions. How can he intend malice if has no idea that he is causing harm, if he cannot imagine properly the effect on us of what he does? To think of consequences, emotional, psychiatric consequences, requires an ability to put oneself in the place of all those others affected by our actions. To have no sense of others as thinking, feeling people, to be innocent as Joe is innocent, may be to live free of vanity, but it may equally lead to a life of breathtaking emotional selfishness.

Joe is baffled by my inability to understand him, expecting me to be wired into his thoughts. 'Ugh,' he'll grunt, pointing nowhere in particular. 'Ugh!'

'What, Joe? What do you want?'

'Well obviously, you idiot parent,' his expression suggests, 'what I want is "ugh"!'

What he's pointing at, I have no idea. It could be just outside the window, it could be miles away. He expects me to know. He seems not to differentiate between his own thoughts and the thoughts he assumes I'll have. Now and then, he'll be sitting on the other side of the room leafing through the pages of a book on his raised knees when he'll jab at something on the page. All I can see is the cover, and not much of that. Joe stabs again and looks up to see if I've cottoned on. I'll walk over and try to tip the book forward to see what's caught his eye. No, he doesn't want me to do that, he wants to keep looking at it himself, but he does want me to say something about the thing on the page in the book in front of him. He jabs again and grunts. It's clear that this is supposed to be sufficient to demand an answer. 'But, Joe,' I want to say pointlessly, 'Daddy can't see what you're looking at. How could I when the book is so obviously turned away from me? I don't look through your eyes, for heaven's sake, I don't have your thoughts.'

Daniel Tammet, whom I once featured in a programme on Radio 4, has recited *pi* from memory to 22,514 decimal places. It took him five hours. He is an amazing, gentle character whose Asperger's comes across as an engaging English timidity. When he was young he went on holiday with another family. Feeling homesick, he rang his mother and asked her to ring him back. Then he put the phone down. 'I didn't realise,' he said, 'that I had to give her the number. I assumed that since I had it, she did too.'

There's a well-known experiment you can try with small children to see if they've acquired a sense of other people's consciousness. I've seen its invention in numerous forms variously attributed to Daniel Dennett, a philosopher, Simon Baron-Cohen, a psychopathologist, and psychologists Heinz Wimmer and Joseph Perner. It goes like this:

Hide a toy in a box while a doll is watching. The doll then goes out of the room. Take the toy out of the box and hide it somewhere else. The doll comes back into the room. Where does she look for her toy? If your child thinks she'll look in the box, then it's evidence of a theory of mind – an understanding that the doll doesn't know the things we do; doesn't know, because she wasn't in the room, that the toy has moved. If the doll looks in the new hiding place, your child is assuming that the knowledge the toy has been moved is somehow universal, that to some extent her own thoughts are everyone's thoughts. The experiment is known as a false-belief task and most children begin to pass by the time they're about four, though some researchers claim to have detected the skill earlier. Even if such a narrative could be presented to Joe, which I doubt, he'd unquestionably fail.

Does he know that hitting is wrong? He's been told so often enough and knows that it will meet disapproval, even felt the painful consequences of bad behaviour when other children hit him back, but I'm not sure that he's worked out the causal relationship. It's sometimes said that morality is simply an internalised fear of punishment. Even if true, we do normally grasp the rationale; we're told why bad behaviour is punished and in general we learn to accept the logic. Joe, I suspect, is still unsure why a punch is wrong, and so any chastisement, any moral rebuke, might well seem arbitrary to him. Morality based on whim would struggle for anyone's assent and so Joe's disdain for it won't feel, as far as he's concerned, wrong.

How aware is Joe of being a living person? As conscious, I imagine, as a fish that it swims in water; namely, not very. He wouldn't care if you put him in a dress. He'd rather be naked, inside the house or out, in company or alone, presumably expecting others to be as comfortable with his naturism as he is. He has no idea that he was born or that he will die. He's not much interested in his own reflection, certainly less so than chimpanzees, who are reportedly fascinated once they realise they're looking at their own image.

He seems to me to exist almost entirely with what he knows and feels there and then. If he is angry, I doubt that he can ever say to himself, as some of us can in our better moments, 'you're angry, calm down'; he simply lives on inside his anger until the moment passes.

This is often what we admire when we talk about the innocence of children – a lack of self-awareness. But are we clear that this implies a lack of awareness for others, that without consciousness of ourselves and all our passions and appetites we'll find it near impossible to imagine the needs, interests, preferences of others? How do we show consideration of other points of view if we expect the world to share ours – indeed, can't imagine that the rest of the world would hold a different one? Adam Smith said it best in *The Theory of Moral Sentiments* in 1759: '… it is by changing places in fancy with the sufferer … that we come either to conceive or to be affected by what he feels …' This mechanism he imagined to be self evident

in every human being 'how selfish soever man may be supposed'. Smith had not the pleasure of knowing autism, and so
never suspected there could be any among us incapable of this
imaginative impersonation. Yet even without that instructive
example he understood with absolute clarity that moral sentiments depend on worldly sensibility.

Reflection must be an elusive pleasure for Joe and self-consciousness, the ability to have thoughts about our thoughts,
is a prerequisite for being able to think about other people's
thoughts. With a limited capacity for one, he cannot hope to
achieve much of the other.

Self-consciousness seems to me to be the beginning of virtue,
not the end. Once we learn to regard our own thoughts and
emotions from a distance, we've achieved a kind of objectiv-
ity, a grossly deficient one usually, I admit, but we've learned
to observe ourselves instead of only to inhabit the thought of
the moment. If we can make judgements about others, taking
the view from there, not only the view from here where we lie
deep inside an instant of our own passion, we become capable
of recognising and acting on their interests, not just our own.
To achieve all this requires a loss of innocence.

For Joe, all the world is his world, and the paradox is that
the more complete his egotism the more innocent it makes
him. He knows little and can imagine little of the corruptions
of my adult mind, because he knows little and can imagine
little of my adult mind, full stop. In most children this fades.
Upholders of innocence regret its passing. But as it fades, it is

supplemented by a growing understanding of the complicated needs and expectations of those around us. We tend to avoid people in whom that doesn't happen. We think them selfish, uncivilised. How peculiar, then, that in children we call this quality innocence and wish to preserve it.

In the Garden of Eden, the shock of knowledge to Adam and Eve is to be embarrassed with self-consciousness. For with that comes shame, a highly complex emotion, and guilt. So should we now want innocence back? Rowan Williams, the Archbishop of Canterbury, argues that it's a fallacy to think we can roll back the wheel to pure innocence. There's no returning to Eden, he says, and quotes Friedrich von Hugel, a Catholic philosopher at the end of the nineteenth century, to the effect that the greatest good for an un-fallen being would be innocence, but the greatest good for a fallen being is forgiveness and reconciliation.

You don't have to believe in the literal truth of The Fall to get the point. Joe's innocence is so unknowing and thus often uncaring that it can be violently hurtful. Perhaps in an uncontaminated world, incapable of sin, innocence would be benign, but it strikes me that much of the harm Joe does is because he is not worldly enough. Forgiveness and reconciliation are the qualities of a mature and experienced mind.

This is clear when we take a special case of moral behaviour that causes philosophers a good deal of trouble precisely because of the problem of self-awareness: altruism.

It's sometimes said that genuine altruism is impossible

because we enjoy some benefit ourselves, even if only the warm glow of doing good, so that self-awareness of our actions trumps altruism, with smug self-satisfaction at best, crudely calculating self-interest at worst. Furthermore, says the Darwinian fundamentalist, altruism can never be truly to our disadvantage or it would have been bred out of us: how could it survive natural selection if it did harm to our genetic prospects?

The standard case for those who disagree with the sceptics is what happens when a group of men sees a child beginning to lose balance over the fence around a well. Before reacting, do they pause to calculate the complicated reciprocal obligations by which they might gain from saving the child? Is their rush to haul her back motivated by self-interest?

Evidently not; there's no time for so much computation. The view either that the rescuers are briskly assessing the child's parents' likely wealth and gratitude, or that they do it because it feels good (and so is selfish really), deserves mocking. The philosopher Mary Midgely obliges delightfully. Even an offer from the most skilled pharmacist to induce such a sensation won't do, she writes: 'Avengers do not want the sensation of avenging; they want people's blood. And similarly, rescuers and benefactors do not (if they are real ones) just want the sensation of rescuing and benefacting. They want to help people. This involves wanting the people actually to be helped.'

Serious Darwinians aren't as crude as some of their bar-room followers and largely concede these points, countering that the computation occurs not in the individual moment, but throughout evolution itself, so that it is not the bystander at the well but natural selection which unconsciously computes the benefit of the altruistic impulse in humanity, and finds it, to some extent in some people, worth preserving.

How do these analyses of altruism stand comparison with Joe's example? If you really want a model of egotism, here he is. But what makes him so? Certainly not an excess of calculation, since Joe barely stops to calculate other people's benefit, being scarcely aware that they are capable even of receiving it. Nor is it an excess of self consciousness that wrecks his altruism by causing him to bask in the pleasure of doing good and so proving himself more interested in self congratulation than helping others. In both cases the problem is, in fact, the very opposite: the absence of calculation, calculation in the moment, and the absence of sufficient self-consciousness are together the fatal blows to Joe's altruism. The surprising conclusion from Joe's example is that he needs more calculation in order to see the consequences of his actions clearly, and he needs more self consciousness in order to explore that internal model of other people's feelings which familiarity with our own feelings provides. Only then might his egotism begin to abate.

If, as I've argued in relation to Joe, it is self-consciousness that makes altruism possible (only by knowing ourselves can we think about what's right for others), how can it also be that the presence of self-consciousness during an act makes altruism impossible? How can the sine qua non of altruism also disqualify it? Some sceptics of altruism seem to me to want to have their cake and eat it; illogical, not to say a little selfish.

What would Joe do watching the child at the well? I suspect he'd not even continue watching. Sympathy or empathy being foreign to him both because of his inability to imagine what others feel and because he's unable to forsee the effect of his actions, so too is he incapable of altruism. It's not the presence of self-consciousness that spoils his altruistic instincts, it's the lack of self-consciousness that means his altruism doesn't even get started; calculation doesn't necessarily render our instincts selfish, but lack of calculation certainly does. And the calculation we need is not one honed in our distant past and the refinement of human instinct on the Savannah, it is explicit calculation, today, here and now, about others.

In order to do good, we have to show an awareness of the effects of our actions without straining to build in a pay-off. That, I think, is the midpoint most of us aspire to, all we have time or inclination for. Egotism sufficiently extreme to be fatal to virtue stands only at the far end of the scale in each direction, either in the ruthless maximisation of self-interest or in utter self absorption to the point of ignorance of others, and few of us reside there. Joe, by comparison, teaches us that we're better than rampant egotists – not in spite of but because of our lost innocence, in part because of our introspection – better than we're sometimes inclined to give ourselves credit for.

It's interesting, though, that Joe does say a kind of sorry. As we made our way from the lift out onto the top floor of the car park after the Great Toddler Incident, I tried yet again with a stern face to tell him that hitting was bad. He raised his hand towards me ... I flinched ever so slightly ... and he stroked my arm with a wide, flat palm, not with gentleness exactly, but calm and conciliatory.

We taught him to do this after he'd been chastised, more as a way of pretending to his sister that he was sorry he'd hurt her than of being sure he really was. I suspect he doesn't know why this makes amends, nor am I quite sure myself; all I can say is that its timidity reaches into my soft heart more surely than any aggression, and Joe knows at least that it stops the big people going on at him in that noisy way of theirs. Somehow, in spite of its innocence, I find myself falling easily into forgiveness and reconciliation.

'It's OK, Joe. It's OK.'

# 9
# Seeing

The phone call at the beginning of term didn't shock, to my surprise, but dulled my spirit with weariness: 'He's broken his front tooth, head-butting the pavement.'

They'd been on the way to a café, a place he likes (a treat, for heaven's sake), when Joe's slow, hopeful haul towards settling in came to grief in splintered enamel. He was not yet ten and it wasn't the first time he'd broken an adult tooth. That small milestone passed at six years old when he twisted face down on a long, steep slide and stood up at the bottom with a jagged hole in the dead centre of his smile, a good-sized triangle chipped from the corner of each front incisor. You have to marvel at the forces at work that day, vandalising with such symmetry. Nearly three hours under general anaesthetic at Great Ormond Street Hospital produced a small work of art by way of repair, rebuilding Joe's teeth without crowns, using synthetic enamel, achieving near-perfect colour match and a join barely visible. He fought like hell as he went under, screaming hysterically as they slid the cannula into a vein in that tiny arm, clamped still under two strong adult hands while I grasped his body, trying with futility to whisper to his pain and rage. In the moment the anaesthetic seeped along his arm and touched his brain, it was as if he had been unplugged. When the rabid resistance simply, swiftly, so uncharacteristically left his body, it felt like death, and I cried helplessly.

Beforehand they said: 'It'll be fine, don't worry, we're used to all sorts of children here.'

Afterwards they said: 'I see what you mean.'

Now he'd been and gone and done it again. Joe had a habit of provoking feeling as oxymoron; in this case, seething pity. It had long been one of his more frustrating tendencies, the unexplained rebellion, the sudden vote to strike, the freeze, common even when favourite destinations beckoned. Though capable of monumental obstinacy, Joe seemed at these moments to be struck by something more, something physical. He looked oddly uncertain, or terrified; he might shout, slip the hold of an adult hand, lean back as we heaved like the anchor in a tug o' war. From time to time and without apparent cause Joe would silently stick; that's how it came to be described, his sticking points. As if suffering the mother of total mechanical breakdowns, his eyes would crease shut and one hand cover his face, the other stretched out to fend off who-knows-what. He'd stick getting out of the car, superglued, one foot in, one foot out, the door wide open in our narrow lane, a rat-run for school traffic which was late, frazzled, and simply made Joe's sticking more vicious by frightening him with impatient hooting. He'd stick halfway across a road, midway through a shop in some chance aisle as if dithering over a purchase, arrested by the bargain of a two-for-one on cornflakes. He'd stick in doorways, a regular inconvenience this one, like the cartoon of the man tying his lace in front of the sliding tube doors, holding back the flood. The resolute little blob stuck on stairs, stuck going from one room to another. It might happen whenever he was in transition and I'd turn round to find him twenty metres adrift, putting down roots.

Our first instinct was to try to persuade – 'Come on, Joe!' – then to wonder if the hand across his eyes meant a headache – 'What's wrong, Joe?' – a problem with bright light, some sudden apprehension? In the end, our habit was to give him half a minute's grace and then a helping hand here, a hustling voice to jolt him awake there, a good shove in those special cases where the looming HGV added incentive for the rest of us, if not for eyes-tight-shut Joe. In his most frozen moments, I bundled him under an arm.

With luck, the incident on the way to the café was no more than another sticking point and not a resurgence of antipathy to the whole regime, or another attempt to bully it. His spontaneity suggested the former, his violence the latter.

What brings Joe so hard against the buffers? In truth, no one knows, but there is a fascinating suspicion to do with the way he sees the world. *The Curious Incident of the Dog in the Night-Time*, by Mark Haddon, an autistic boy's detective story, is an exuberant, thrilling work of imagination. Its central character, Christopher, is a James Bond among autistics: astonishing, improbable, an artistic creation beyond the bounds of life, but captivating all the same. Moreover, the book achieves the impossible by deriving narrative drive from a character who would typically have only the weakest grasp of psychological motivation. Nevertheless, there are moments of brilliant, speculative insight. One such is when Christopher arrives at Paddington after running away from his father's house and steps out of the train into the sensory storm of a mainline railway station:

> When I saw how big the room was that the train was in and I heard how noisy and echoey it was I had to kneel down on the ground for a bit because I was going to fall over … I groaned to block out the noise and I looked around the big room at all the signs to see if this was London. And the signs said:

> Sweet pastries **Heathrow Airport Check-In Here** *Bagel Factory* **EAT** *excellence and taste* YO! sushi! **Stationlink** Buses **WHSmith** MEZZANINE Heathrow Express **Clinique** First Class Lounge FULLERS **easyCar.com** *The Mad Bishop* **and Bear Public House** Fuller's London Pride Dixons **Our Price** Paddington Bear at Paddington Station **Tickets Taxis** …

And so on for more than half a page. Christopher closes his eyes and counts to fifty 'because my brain wasn't working very well'. The suggestion is that he has an attention to the detail of visual images so scrupulous that each and every one of them leaves a perfect fingerprint on Christopher's memory, and that so much visual information for one so receptive causes an overload. We're all half guessing what goes on in the brains of autistic children, but this computer-crash of the mind is a vivid image. Could it be that some such overwhelming sensory cascade is part of Joe's experience that helps explain why he sticks?

I wouldn't call his visual memory photographic but it is certainly exceptionally good. My father used to ask, as all fathers ask at the end of a long journey, 'Do you know where you are yet?' 'No,' we would say, looking but not seeing, dumbfounded, as we rounded the last-but-one corner before home. Joe always knows. By about the age of five I should think he knew every street for miles around and these days I suspect he's mastered the contour of pretty much every hill between here and Bristol. It used to worry me that one of his escapes might take him confidently to Sainsbury's in Watford, four miles away. My hunch is that he learnt how to spell by remembering each word as an elaborate shape, noting the way the letters formed its lumps and sticks and curves, because he certainly didn't do it by remembering larger, more manageable pieces of phonetics. If we imagine a continuum of perspective, intricate detail at one end and the global view at the other, Joe seems to lie well towards a preference for the bitty.

'What if,' asks Uta Frith, 'complex information received by the senses was not processed in the same way by children with autism?' Her question is a tease, since it suggests that we can learn about the manner of our own perception by contrasting it with those like Joe who may be an indication that there are other ways of organising what we see.

If that sounds preposterous, if it seems obvious that we see what's there, pretty much as it appears, it's worth considering a theory of autism Frith helped develop with Francesca Happe, known as 'weak central coherence'. The name is descriptive: central coherence is the capacity to draw together detail to form a whole so that, for instance, the pieces of a jigsaw cease to be individual pieces once we see the completed picture. Weak coherence, she says, means that the picture never quite coalesces in the mind, means not seeing the whole for the parts, the wood for the trees. An over strong central coherence, on the other hand, might mean not seeing the trees for the wood. Ordinarily, surprisingly perhaps, most of us seem to pick the same units to parcel up the outside world, because, as Frith acknowledges, it would be possible to choose a level of detail a good deal smaller than a tree: a branch, a leaf even, the stepped edges of a single leaf, failing to see the trees for the twigs. We're quite capable of consciously moving between these levels by refocusing our attention, but most of the time we don't have to, the eyes of any crowd lurking in much the same focal range. At some level, even autistic children ignore the ever-finer degrees of minutiae into which they could, conceivably, descend, but they do seem inclined to concentrate on smaller bits than the rest of us. At last, someone who'd actually prefer the crumbs at the bottom of the crisp bag.

Joe, like many others with autism, is good at jigsaws, though has little enthusiasm for them. Frith suggests this is because he will always have an aptitude for identifying fragments. There's experimental evidence to show that children with autism perform better than normal children at tasks requiring attention to what's called embedded detail – pictures or shapes hidden within larger pictures. She argues, rightly in my view, that this could be seen as a strength, and anyone who has gawped at Joe's ability to fly through the visual cacophony in a shop display of several hundred videos and pick out, in seconds, the one he wants, recognises a rare perceptive talent. While my eyes dart about, unable to focus easily on single titles, trying stupidly to take in the rows of tapes as a whole, his sweep smoothly and rapidly over the surface of typefaces and colours as if hoovering up detail in speed.

This suggests, maybe to our surprise, that how we see is an act of unconscious choice as well as a simple physical perception, a cognitive style, as Frith and Happe put it. We must be continually giving our visual perception some kind of guidance, but what kind? And where from? Frith suggests a source and the beginnings of a second theory known as 'executive function':

Psychologists have long distinguished 'bottom-up' and 'top-down' processes in the complex handling of incoming stimuli. The former process is controlled by incoming data, the latter by previous experience. A few decades ago, many psychologists assumed that bottom-up processes had priority. Now the general consensus is that top-down processes continuously modulate the bottom-up flow of incoming information. For instance, previous experience establishes whether incoming stimuli are expected or unexpected. If they are expected, then they are automatically processed more thoroughly. In this way the onslaught of the mass of incoming stimuli can be controlled. In autism this type of control might be lacking.

It's been suggested that one consequence of this deficit is an inability to shift attention easily from one scene to another, from Joe's house at school, perhaps, to the street outside on the way to the café, from the car to the front door in the lane in our village.

In *The Curious Incident* when Christopher faces that sensory blitzkrieg at Paddington station, he is, of course, confronted with nothing more or less than the rest of us negotiate with relative ease. Some might find it a bit of a muddle the first time, but by and large we sail through places like this, quickly discriminating between sensory data that is useful for our purposes and that which isn't: train information rather than fast food if we've no time to lose, the sign for the lavatory rather than the cash machine. This is processing capacity of ruthless efficiency, and yet most of the time we're barely conscious of much more than a flitting of the eyes and a homing instinct.

'What is it that attunes attention?' asks Frith. 'How do we know what is important so that we can attend to it? Some high-level "executive" component in the mind has to decide what in the mass of incoming sensations is worth attending to.'

She is surely right that we seem to have some kind of top-down faculty that helps us burn through the sensory equivalent of junk mail. In a series of extraordinary tests, it has been shown that we screen out any information that doesn't seem relevant to a predetermined purpose. This is so even when the information might ordinarily be expected to gatecrash our attention.

Daniel Simons and Daniel Levin conducted an experiment in which people on a college campus were stopped and asked by a stranger for directions. Ten or fifteen seconds into their conversation, two men walked between them carrying a wooden door, momentarily obscuring the line of sight between subject and stranger. Once the door passed and the conversation resumed, the stranger had been substituted for another, dressed differently, of different height, different build and with a different voice. Half those taking part failed to notice any difference. We can speculate that people felt their purpose was to impart information to a stranger, which they pursued with such determination that it obscured the fact that the stranger metamorphosed before them.

In another now famous experiment a group of people was shown a tape of a basketball game and asked to count the passes by one side. About half failed to notice that a woman dressed in a gorilla suit walked slowly across the court for nine seconds, turning at one point to face the camera and beat her chest. If the viewers were given no task to perform, other than simply watching the game, they noticed the 'gorilla' straight away.

It's evident, then, that our attention is ruthlessly directed by our purposes. We rationalise, force it to comply with some stringent contextual rule. We screen, we filter, we don't so much ignore because we don't even seem to notice that there *is* anything to ignore; we simply disregard visual stimuli by the bucketful, behaving as if what interests us is all there is, and we do so without trying or even being aware of what we're doing.

Is it plausible that Joe, lacking that ruthless executive telling him what not to take in, tries to digest the whole lot? And that furthermore, lacking a sense of how the whole lot forms a single picture, he tries to take in the whole lot at a deep level of detail? This is a claim implied elsewhere in *The Curious Incident* and sounds to me, at least, like just the thing to induce a breakdown. If true, sticking or freezing would be no surprise, for what he would be attempting is breathtaking. It could be likened to the nightmarish feeling of being lost, late and perhaps drunk in a heaving city we think we ought to know, staring down every route from the crossroads where we stand panicking, scanning the myriad grains of visual texture, nothing recognisable, assailed by noise, scratching for some clue to our whereabouts but finding none. Incapable of making a choice amid the chaos of sensory data, we crumble.

It would be for Joe and others as for Temple Grandin, who writes that 'when noise and sensory over-stimulation became too intense, I was able to shut off my hearing and retreat into my own world'. Others with autism speak of an occasional oversensitivity to light, noise or bustling activity. So though it is a cognitive style with undoubted advantages at times, perhaps it can also feel like rawness, a tenderness easily inflamed.

In his book *The Man Who Mistook His Wife for a Hat*, Oliver Sacks describes a patient, Jose, an autistic boy aged twenty-one said to be hopelessly retarded but with an extraordinary gift for drawing. He was capable of reproducing objects with remarkable fidelity, but more than this, his pictures showed wit and imagination. He was an artist.

And yet the peculiarity of his art, says Sacks, was that it remained rooted in the particular. At one point, Sacks speculates that some of the drawings might have had symbolic meanings, a large fish and a smaller one leaping together from the sea being perhaps himself and Jose, for example. I find this improbable, and in any case, somewhat in contradiction, Sacks goes on to comment in quite different terms on the fastidious, botanical exactness of Jose's first drawing for many years from life, of a dandelion:

His mind is not built for the abstract, the conceptual. That is not available to him as a path to truth. But he has a passion and a real power for the particular – he loves it, he enters into it, he recreates it. And the particular, if one is particular enough, is also a road – one might say nature's road – to reality and truth.

The particular is in certain respects at odds with the symbolic. If a picture shows essentially this subject, this scene, this particular flower, it is hard to see how it also reaches beyond the particular to some other essence. If your fish are particular, then these fish are these fish, not analogies of human relationships. So Sacks seems to me on more consistent ground when he continues:

> The abstract, the categorical, has no interest for the autistic person – the concrete, the particular, the singular is all. Whether this is a question of capacity or disposition, it is strikingly the case. Lacking, or indisposed to, the general, the autistic seem to compose their world picture entirely of particulars. Thus they live, not in a universe but in what William James calls a "multiverse", of innumerable, exact and passionately intense particulars.

We spent several years teaching Joe intensively using a technique known as applied behavioural analysis, increasingly popular with the parents of children with autism, but relentless and exhausting, taking anything up to forty hours a week of one-to-one instruction. The child's attention is directed wherever possible by an adult – no childish curiosity can be depended on for motivation – and there are strict rules about the management of behaviour. The main educating principle of ABA is that everything to be learnt is broken down into component parts and the lesson repeated innumerable times until, it is hoped, an idea sinks in. For example, we taught Joe prepositions – in, on, under, next to – by repeated demonstration with toy animals. The programme did bring certain benefits and there are reports of dramatic improvement in some children, but our biggest problem was that he found great difficulty in carrying these detailed lessons into any wider, more general context. It was as if what he learnt at the table-top was a particular that applied nowhere else. Thus 'next to' was a concept he never quite grasped except in relation to a certain plastic sheep and cow, and even then it was possible he responded to the visual prompt of seeing these animals rather than the spoken words denoting their arrangement. Paul Bloom makes the ruthless comment that 'a perfect memory, one that treats experience as a distinct thing-in-itself, is useless'.

To be 'local' in the extreme would leave us lost in William James's 'multiverse'. To be entirely global would be, in words that sound like sentimental piety, to conceive all we see as one. No one is so unfortunate as to languish at either end, we all sit somewhere on a continuum, but I find it unsettling and odd, liquefying my foundations, to think that the way I see works on a scale that others might not share.

I can be as clear about the video I want as Joe, yet Joe is an order of magnitude better than me at spotting it. Even when seeking things about which he's not that fanatical – yoghurts on the supermarket shelf, for example – he makes me feel like a perceptual sloth. His visual memory is vastly superior to mine, his eye for detail sharper. Sometimes, when sitting down, he'll stop, pick up and throw away a single crumb from the chair.

It's plausible, given Joe's disabilities, that he might need a different perceptual strategy. If you find it hard to categorise, if, as seems to be true of Joe, your imagination struggles to stretch to the abstract and thus to generalisation, it strikes me that you'd be short of a few of the necessary tools for effective filtering. If, on the other hand, you seem to have an eye for fragments and details, if you seem to be better at identifying component parts rather than aggregating them into the whole, I suppose you might conceivably try to get along by processing as many particulars as you can cram into your eye. I hesitate to embrace that conclusion not only because there have been one or two unresolved theoretical and experimental problems with the idea of central coherence, but partly because in this extreme interpretation of its effects I find what it describes overwhelming. Can it be true?

Anyone who has seen the astonishing drawings of Stephen Wiltshire would find it less incredible, for they are the incredible made real. Often drawn quickly from memory, frequently featuring architectural landmarks, cityscapes, or classic American cars, they have a detailed exactness that is stupefying. His last retrospective exhibition was called 'Not a Camera'.

The title was an insistence that his work has character and personality as well as astonishing fidelity, and all this is true; but it is the quality of intricate precision that first compels our attention. Stephen at work is described not so much looking at a scene as consuming it with apparently casual but breath-taking swiftness and intensity, and by Oliver Sacks as bestowing on one of his subjects, 'a brief, indifferent glance', before reproducing it with style and exactitude.

And as Stephen reproduces on paper the images taken in with such accuracy, the same process seems to be at work in reverse, the details racing out. A past president of the Royal Academy, Sir Hugh Casson, said of him: 'From the first mark the pencil moves as quickly and as surely as a sewing-machine – the line spinning from the pencil point like embroidery.'

In the introduction to Stephen's book *American Dream*, Margaret Hewson wrote: 'I should like to suggest, albeit tentatively, that autistic artistic savants "see" everything without necessarily focusing upon anything in particular. The vision of lesser mortals is unconsciously highly selective.'

The savant is not as common among autistics as often supposed. People of Stephen's ability are extremely rare, but one or other more moderately heightened skill might still be present in about one in ten with autism, and in many cases their abilities do seem to depend on a highly discriminating eye or ear or memory for detail. A cognitive style that prefers the local to the global, the detail to the whole, might extend to many more than the savants. It is unquestionably an impressive talent.

Why doesn't the mind normally work this way, asks the psychologist Paul Bloom. 'Why don't we store each instance as a precious and unique individual ...? One answer is that all of these discrete memories could not fit into our heads.' That's not quite good enough, as Bloom agrees, because we don't know if capacity is a problem, we don't know what the human capacity for discrete mental impressions is. The deeper explanation is that detail holds us up when we're busy determining the broad categorisation of things around us, and it is by swift categorisation that we recognise those things; limiting the detail makes the world comprehensible. Regard the chair in its uniqueness, in all its detailed particulars, with no reference to any category, and you might dwell on the grain of the wood or the texture of the plastic and scarcely be aware that it's a chair at all, might not even appreciate that it can be sat on. Oliver Sacks's man who mistook his wife for a hat, Dr P, a musician of distinction, was probably as close to such a case as one can get, seeing only detail and never the whole, and describing a glove as 'a continuous surface, infolded on itself ... five outpouchings, if that is the word'.

Maybe autistic children sometimes find themselves, if not at such an extreme, then not far from it, perhaps momentarily overwhelmed by particulars. When moving between one place and another, especially from one atmospheric light into another, perhaps Joe carries a jigsaw of the world in his hands which never quite fuses into a whole and, for a moment or two, in the haste to assemble a new jigsaw of a new scene, the pieces fall and scatter. When I think of him, nervy and tentative as I step blithely from one scene to another, pulling his hand, I wonder how I could ever again be impatient of a boy who sometimes finds himself among scenes of infinite broken eggshell.

How much easier, we might think, to swan along picking up no more than the gist of what's going on around us. More than seventy years ago, Professor F. C. Bartlett said of the results of a famous series of experiments on memory that an individual does not usually take in a situation detail by detail. 'In all ordinary instances,' said Bartlett, 'he has an overmastering tendency simply to get a general impression of the whole; and, on the basis of this, he constructs the probable detail.' That is, recollection is very much that: we remember the broad outline and then gather the pieces we think most likely to have been present. We do not even attempt to store them all. The surprising conclusion is that sometimes perceptual laziness can also have its advantages, one of which is a kind of cognitive economy, a second that it makes the world recognisable, and a third being our own composure: if our world were prone to disintegration, it would be no surprise if we were too.

Quite likely Joe will always stick from time to time, whether at school or home, and the rest of us will fight our impatience, reminding ourselves as we call 'Come on, Joe!' repeatedly to the child who has apparently just gone on sullen strike that this is not necessarily borne of wilfulness. Whether the theory is right, that he feels as if someone has just rattled his mosaic, we might never know for sure, but I'm inclined to try at least to give him the benefit of the doubt.

A few weeks later Great Ormond Street worked its magic on his smile once more. He woke up to become briefly preoccupied by the novel sensation in his mouth, trying, but failing, to pull off the new piece of tooth. We had managed the anaesthetic better too, and he went out on gas with far less ferocious panic.

And as term progressed, a strange thing happened: the reports took a sudden turn for the better. Joe, we heard, had become more compliant, he began to participate more fully in the routines and rituals of school life. He was joining in with the singing before meals, he performed his household chores with something approaching enthusiasm. He had whole weeks of cheerful, playful cooperation. If this episode had been another blaze of resentment, then it seemed to be subsiding, at last. Perhaps the fight was going out of him here too. Perhaps it had been no less a rebellion than the fearful one against that earlier anaesthetic, just more protracted. Perhaps now, I dared think, they had been able to whisper to his rage in that gentle, persistent way of theirs and convince him that he could find comfort and familiarity among them. Maybe, at last, some of the new pieces were beginning to settle.

# 10
# Meaning

What are we to make of Joe and how should we treat him? These pages have invited reflection on a range of commonplace but amazing human capacities – all described in direct contrast to Joe. Allow me a deep breath, for having chased that contrast so far, I've found myself up a garden path facing some thorny questions: if Joe shows our most distinguishing features in such sharp relief, is he still one of us? If I accept the arguments of philosophers that we define ourselves as humans not in the Linnaean fashion by our appearance but rather by what goes on in our heads, then I'm forced to a grim conclusion: Joe, my son, does not qualify.

Humans have rich self-consciousness, says philosophy; Joe, quite likely in my view, does not. Humans have sophisticated moral codes; the case for Joe's innocence is that he does not. Humans have language or, better still, deep structured language; Joe does not. Humans have elaborate culture, indeed they continually remake their own culture at an express rate, including their own history. I have never managed to share with Joe any communication about the past, and its singular purpose in him, such as it is, seems to be to reinforce habit and

obsession. Culture has been found to be the feeblest of humanity's distinguishing characteristics as a vast array of creatures,
from birds to dolphins and other primates, turns out to share
and pass on cultural understandings. If we restrict ourselves to
saying that humans have higher culture – art, literature and
the like – then Joe, once more, does not.

I confess, as I said at the outset, that this problem gives my
head some trouble, though my heart – following a less pon-
derous course – couldn't care less for my head's pretentious
scruples. Come off it, says heart, Joe is your son. Ah, but you
need more robustly objective measures than that, says head.
Oh, sod all that, says heart. And yet I would like to reconcile
heart and mind, in favour of my heart naturally, but preferably
with something approaching intellectual respectability. How
to do it?

In my case, by wandering through the main gate at Emmanuel
College, Cambridge, five years ago. Emma's low-rise sandstone
quadrangles lack the huddled, lowering insularity of don-dom,
and breathe the beeping diesel air of the bus station next door.
Few pretensions, Emma, even the name being abbreviated to
sound like a friend. It still strikes me as less aloof than most
– nothing to do, I suspect, with either architecture or residents,
but down to the three years I spent at the place just along
the road. We were neighbours, and though I knew few of its
students and seldom visited, Emma suggests to me even now a
still-remembered hospitality from the times we lumbered late
at night onto the slippery floor of a strip-lit basement bar for
frothy pints in shivering plastic glasses.

So I arrived cheerfully that day to see an academic vicar who had very publicly ceased to believe in God some years previously, then survived a subsequent campaign to defrock him. In spite of his now long-acknowledged atheism, it was as if a spiritual poke in the ribs kept him awake at night. In the years since declaring God dead, he'd found himself unable to go the whole hog and embrace unvarnished materialism, but spent the time instead continuing to call himself a vicar and labouring to name his metaphysical itch, trying in all modesty to redefine religion. In the year or two before I met him, he'd tended towards a variation of nature worship but seemed half-hearted in this conviction as in others. He was a man of spirit undergoing refurbishment, like the shell of a shop, not much on sale. Being uneasy with certainty myself, I knew how he felt.

I was interviewing him for a programme about the durability of religion, and he was delightful: thoughtful and honest, trying painfully to give substance to a feeling too airy to be nailed down. Afterwards we had lunch together in one of the cheerful cafés along St Andrew's Street where taste had mattered to us as students less than calorific value.

'Do you have a family?' he wondered. I told him the basics. He inquired further. Whenever I find myself describing Joe to someone for the first time he comes out sounding odd and troublesome. Watching the effect of Joe's short story on the vicar across the table, I wondered whether he'd attempt a rationale with whatever kind of theology still worked for him. He did.

'Oh, bad luck,' he said. 'Bad luck.'

And that was it. He stared down into his plate and gently, silently shook his head. I wondered for some time afterwards if that was the limit of spiritual consolation in his cosmos or if he was simply avoiding the awkwardness of saying something trite to someone he presumed had tired of hearing patronising consolations years ago, or then again if it was meant as a kind of sensitivity – 'let's not dwell on such sorrow'. I think now it was probably all three. 'Bad luck' seemed to be the sum of meaning he attached to Joe's life.

'Bad luck.'

Is that it? I thought, and my bad luck at that, not Joe's?

I make no secret of my desire for meaning. But there are risks in such wishful vanity. One is the hideous peril of falling for Hollywood-grade philosophising about mental disability and the cloying redemption of films like *I Am Sam* or *Forrest Gump* in which invariably sweet-natured simpletons are put on earth to do the rest of us good. God wants it that way, it's implied. They're *useful*, these people, like Swiss army knives for the soul. One has to resist the temptation to think that Joe's value lies in therapy for the rest of us, a gift to help us rise above the trivial gripes of our spoilt lives.

Hollywood is at one solipsistic extreme, 'bad luck' used to strike me as being at the other, both essentially relegating Joe to the role of bit player in the lives of others. He is either the bad in my luck or a guide to self-improvement.

I have changed my mind, not about Hollywood, but about 'bad luck'. 'Bad luck' now seems to me a persuasive and concise statement of the case to include Joe in the human community, though we need to be clear that it's Joe's luck we're talking about.

One of the most articulate advocates of this line of argument is Kenan Malik. He is that rare thing these days, a humanist who retains faith in reason, faith in the ability of people to rise above nature, despite a limpid understanding of the science of genetics. He thinks about Darwinism and human nature with rare sophistication.

Part of his answer to the problem of how to address serious mental disability is that we regard these people as being like us because they once had the *potential* to be like us. Potential is a useful thought. It idealises humanity and claims there's a germ of the ideal in us all. That Platonic promise, though cruelly frustrated in the event, should nevertheless be taken as a determining factor in our identity. And if, by bad luck, potential is savagely unrealised, it should make no difference to our fundamental moral judgements of one another, since to some extent we all fall short.

But potential has problems too. It reminds me of the Jane Austen character who could have been a great pianist, if only she played. Potential, it may be argued, is nothing if not realised. If, as seems likely, Joe's problems are genetically based, he may have been potentially like us only when he existed before conception as a nice idea. 'It could have been different, if only it was different.' Yeah, right. 'I could have been a contender.' Sure. We might regret what might have been, but we don't often end our judgement there. On the contrary, we forget potential with surprising ease in favour of the pianist who actually plays.

The philosopher Mary Midgley writes: 'If we contrast a world in which life is still going on, though it will soon cease, with one in which actual life is permanently extinguished, but the seed stores and the sperm banks remain untouched forever, we cannot intelligibly say that the real value lies in the second. Potentiality only matters because of what will happen when it is actualised. Could we think of the blueprints as more important than the building, the mix than the pudding, the match than the fire?'

More important? No. And yet ... suddenly I feel an unreasonable sympathy for the match that won't strike.

Midgley must be right that potential is not the only or even the most important test, but it surely plays a part. It draws on sentiments notoriously hard to extinguish: hope and expectation. They thrive before conception as much as after. Even if time has rendered them futile, their memory lingers, and memories make identities too. We hold on to them with phrases like 'I once hoped ...', and even though the hope be dashed, it remains expressive of us that we once held it, and descriptive of the child of whom we hoped. For me, the non-striking match genuinely belongs to the class of things that are meant to burn brightly, and the gulf between potential and unfulfilled event fills with a pity almost too great to bear. Those seed stores forever untouched are an image of pure agony, and their potential stays with us whatever their ultimate fate. Why define entirely by accident rather than design? There is, I think, some place for potential in the measure of others, far into the past though it may have died. And if potential has been frustrated? Well then, 'bad luck' is all the difference. This thin phrase, casual in everyday use, does not diminish Joe; rather it shows how narrow is the gap between us.

But I think there is an even better case for Joe than frustrated potential. It comes, inadvertently, from Francis Spufford who we met in an earlier chapter as a wonderful anthropologist of the story. He writes in his autobiography of childhood, *The Boy that Books Built*, about his younger sister, who had the kind of chronic illness that consumed his parents' energy and attention but led him to retreat from her into books. She was allergic to food and so had to be kept on a diet that held her just above starvation while provoking her immune system as little as possible, trailing tubes and wires wherever she went.

'Ever since,' says Spufford, 'I've hated vulnerable people ... It's the slow people, the learning disabled, the much-euphemised fucked-of-wit I find unbearable, locked in their innocence, tottering through a world they don't understand in the misplaced confidence that it's safe.'

He remembers seeing on the bus a twenty-year-old girl with some undefined mental disability.

'I would have taken away what afflicted her if I could,' he says, 'but since I couldn't I hated her for what she made me feel and wished her dead, or at least segregated somewhere where the sight of her didn't burrow at the long-buried roots in me of an intolerable pity: a pity I can't live up to and can't bear to be reminded of.'

The attitude, apparently hostile, is intriguing. For when Spufford talks of hating, or turning away, it isn't others he hates, but what they show him of his own frail humanity.

'I loved my little sister,' he says, 'and felt that I owed such a lot of attention to her state that I had better pay none.'

This, to borrow an analogy, is Caliban staring in the mirror. There lurks somewhere in Spufford a sense of how he should appear but doesn't, a duty perhaps, a standard of behaviour that he finds too onerous and so hates the sight of himself for failing to uphold. What is intriguing is the power of this sense to induce so much self-loathing. He doesn't hate his sister, he hates himself for turning away from her. Some powerful moral archetype plays hell with Spufford's self-respect. He calls this archetype pity. I suggested duty, but on reflection I think it's quite simply fellow feeling. I doubt that he feels with the same intensity the same pity for animals. No, it's the specifically human vulnerability he hates. Bravely admitting that he was unable to rise to it tells us what he thinks humanity should normally expect of itself.

And what is that? I sense it is that Spufford feels that his sister's humanity depends on him, and maybe that's enough to frighten anyone.

Having called Spufford a Caliban, I'd better admit that the same feeling ravages me from time to time too. My life with Joe is not all about love, and when love seems exhausted what sometimes keeps me dutiful is not pure devotion but fear of the vicious remorse I'd know if I too, having so little excuse, turned my back on Joe. There's not much credit in guilt but it can keep you in attendance when times are hard.

But to call it guilt and leave it at that doesn't begin to do justice to the notion of fellow feeling. Nor does it tell us what we'd be guilty of. There's something more.

I think John Hapgood, the former Archbishop of York, gets close. In his book *Being a Person* he writes that 'personhood is not just a quality, or a set of qualities, given to us. It is a state of being rooted in, and developing through mutual interaction with other persons.'

His central thesis, though he makes no claim to originality, is that we are defined not by our biology alone, but also by our relationships. As he suggests, the notion has been around for a while, given arguably its most lop-sided expression by Karl Marx, who suggests that human nature is entirely social. 'The human essence of nature exists only for *social* man,' wrote Marx, 'for only here does nature exist for him as a bond with other men, as his existence for others and their existence for him, as the vital element of human reality; only here does it exist as the basis of his own human existence.'

Hapgood, writing in 1997, prefers to take his quotations from John Macmurray, a Scottish philosopher. In his 1954 Gifford lectures, Macmurray said:

> We need one another to be ourselves. This complete and unlimited dependence of each of us upon the others is the central and crucial fact of personal existence. Individual independence is an illusion; and the independent individual, the isolated self, is a nonentity. In ourselves we are nothing; and when we turn our eyes inward in

search of ourselves we find a vacuum … It is only in relation to others that we exist as persons; we are invested with significance by others who have need of us; and we borrow our reality from those who care for us. We live and move and have our being not in ourselves but in one another; and what rights or powers or freedom we possess are ours by the grace and favour of our fellows. Here is the basic fact of our human condition.

Macmurray enjoyed a revival in the same year, 1997, when he was said to be Tony Blair's favourite philosophical reading and Blair wrote an introduction to a Macmurray anthology. Whether the philosopher's influence on the politician has been apparent is not something I want to go into. And in any case, these left-ish associations need not imply that the social underpinning of our nature must end in collectivism and higher taxes. Relationships are private affairs too, and so to call us social beings who are defined by relationships is only to assert that we all make better sense when seen with others; it is not to determine the character of those relationships, or who they're with.

As Hapgood points out, Macmurray, like Marx, also goes too far: we need to *be* something before we can relate, but it is a position to which one can grant a little overstatement, for so far have we been influenced by a perverse notion of genetics as implying some kind of chronic individualism that we sometimes lose the sense of humankind as also essentially composed of social beings. No respectable Darwinian actually believes the full human being is a genetic atom, or that our social lives are created by genetics with one-directional causation. Not even the brilliantly but unfortunately named selfish gene can function in isolation in a hostile environment. As the eighteenth-century philsophical bishop Joseph Butler put it, we must resist 'the speculative absurdity of considering ourselves single and independent beings'. We need to loosen just a little the garrotting notion of individual substance. We need to resist the temptation to elect one facet of life, one biological snippet, and declare it life's purpose when there are so many to choose from. In fact, none of the philosophical distinctions with which we began this chapter makes sense if seen as defining us from the inside alone, as if the gift for language is a biological capacity without social purpose, as if the necessary neurons sprang into being and thrived without some conducive environment, to idle away the millennia in nothing more than self-congratulation, the irrelevant fruit of one double helix to the next, as if language even has meaning except in a social context, as if culture is the eternal, unshared property of individuals.

The traditional definitions of humanity mostly reach outwards, yet strangely often without acknowledging what is out there to reach; namely, other people. Yes, we have language to an extraordinary and probably unique degree of complexity, but what for? What else but because there are others to talk to?

Joe may not think so but he needs human society, he could exist in no other. His daily routine is largely set by others, his desires are facilitated (or not) by others, his needs are by and large answered by others. His survival depends on us and even his most idiosyncratic behaviour has evolved among the sparks of abrasion against others. As Macmurray said: 'There are few things that I desire to do … which do not depend upon the active cooperation of others … I need you in order to be myself.'

Since relationships flow in at least two directions, the conclusion for Joe is as follows: he is defined partly by those who have relationships with him, not by himself alone, but also by me, by his carers, his family and those who know him, by what we do with him, for him, to him. It's not practical help for children like Joe at which Francis Spufford winces, it's the sense that their humanity depends on him and his own depends on accepting them. That massive obligation would alarm anyone. Easier perhaps to wish it would go away.

And lest it be thought that the definition goes in only one direction, that Joe, wanting certain characteristics himself, is defined with our help but that we are already defined by ourselves quite without his, recall once more his mind-blindness. Without ever having confronted it, I believe, we would never have understood so much of the richness of our own consciousness or how it worked. We were not inclined to reflect on what often seems obvious as thoroughly as we now do until autism showed us it wasn't obvious at all. I once flattered myself that I was self-aware, before I knew Joe, but I had scant awareness of the way I understood others. I'm a little better acquainted with myself now and have Joe to thank, for one of the greatest aids to self-understanding is the differences in others who give us something to compare. If we need them, as Macmurray says, to be ourselves, we also need them to know ourselves.

There is an African saying that goes: 'It takes a whole village to raise a child.' And so it should. Being 'human' is as collective a label as ever there was.

# Postscript

As I write, Joe is sitting on the carpet, playing *The Cat in The Hat* on his computer, cackling wickedly as the cat and the cake and the rake and the ball come tumbling down. He's just had breakfast of beans on toast and is pestering for Jacob's cream crackers:

'Bik-kit.'

Biscuit.

'Bik-kit.'

It's his latest dietary fad, but a *latest* fad is progress: it means he's added to the old ones. He eats like a food processor, as before, from hand through churning jaws to boundless gullet at a rate of knots, but get this: he also eats – with gusto – salmon, sausage rolls, brown rice, curry, salads … just about everything on the menu. 'Good luck,' I'd said, but they'd side-stepped chance and ganged up on him with iron perseverance instead.

When he comes home he'd still rather exist on Sainsbury's spinach and ricotta tortellini, he is still obsessive and we have to stand our ground. His life's repertoire has expanded but we know it's on a vicious piece of elastic, liable to contract without warning. Still, the sense I had of Joe disappearing into a singularity, an ever-diminishing core of endlessly repeated behaviour, a black hole, is eased thanks to the school's continual efforts to widen his horizons. When he's dropped off there after a weekend or holiday at home, he's calm and I suspect not too far from content.

In other ways, he's the same as ever. He can still, frankly, be an almighty pain in the arse, at school no less than at home. He goes on, and on, as he always did. He's obstinate, unpredictable and occasionally violent. Mind you, it's a good while since I saw him hit anyone else, alert though we remain around crying babies. At times, I continue to feel like a loosely woven cloth out of which Joe strips, strand by strand, most of the fabric until the warp and weft disintegrate and all that's left is a couple of dribbling threads. His carers tell us from time to time, with a smile, how he's been 'a bit difficult' this week, or 'brilliant' the next. Odd new idiosyncrasies sprout from nowhere, he has his ups and downs.

He makes slow but steady developmental progress. He's been picking up a few more words here and there. He seems a little more patient, or maybe it's because he's with me less often that I've gained some patience myself. The occasional change of staff at school rattles him and he does his best to test incomers to destruction. In these periods, at times when I catch Joe staring into space, I can't help wondering if he's plotting their downfall. It still seems possible the whole project could unwind.

So there is no ending, happy or otherwise, but certain fears have receded and new ones emerged. He seems to be moving prematurely into adolescence with excellent potential for disaster as he expresses his maturing self with such a thin sense of social convention. On the whole society tends to crack down on acts like the indecent exposure he's sometimes inclined to. In a toddler we think it cute, in a young adult, arrestable. He has yet to discover girls but, if he does, God knows what will follow – anything, I imagine, from comedy and heartache to real alarm. Still, if all goes well, Joe will be at the school until he's eighteen.

And then what? Frankly, no idea, but just at the moment eight years in which he's at home little more than a quarter of the time feels like an eternity of respite, sometimes too much of an eternity. I tend not to see Joe's future as a steady march to the sunlit uplands, his life doesn't await maturity, change being so slow that I've thought of him for a long time now as of no age in particular. The future is here, it will be as it already is.

I do, though, have a dream, one day in the blue, when Joe sits proudly on my shoulders. A great crowd, as if acclaiming the FA Cup raised in the giant-killing hands of part-time butchers and bakers, cheers euphorically at the perfect realisation of unreasonable hope. It's a dream of a dream fulfilled.

I gesture for calm, the adoring masses settle. I tell them: 'Here he is: Joe. Look upon him, and learn,' and the roar of triumphant acclaim overwhelms us. Hail the glory of Joe! As the reverential hush returns, they strain to gather the words of their philosopher king. And he says:

'Pat!'

'Noo!'

'Pak!'

And I interpret: 'People, Joe says unto you, "A video of Post-man Pat and then Sainsbury's spinach and ricotta tortellini!"' And the cheers echo to the heavens.

It's good comedy, parental vanity, or deserves to be. In defence, no Hollywood starlet falls into my arms in the last scene, but Joe and I bask in teen-fantasy righteousness while before us doubters wither.

Interpretation of this dream is easy: it's a thirst for redemption, for us both. Perhaps that's what this book has been about: I feel Joe has been shut away and that I played a part in shutting him there, so I want to take him out, show him off, claim for him all the interest and importance that his miserly condition would deny, and to do so partly by saying that we can understand ourselves better if only we understand him. So I pull on your sleeve for attention. All books have a bit of the brat about them – look at me, look at me! – this one perhaps more than most.

Although to say that he is shut away is a slander. Joe's carers strive to give him a social life and to some extent succeed. He is, as he should be, part of a wider community now and I feel his own identity grows with his circle of acquaintance. He is not shut away from care and compassion or contact with his neighbourhood where the school is cheerfully accepted, or his family. It's not a bin, unlike some other institutions that once loomed Joe's way, where mere containment is a notable achievement.

Joe was lucky. Rejection by his school wasn't far away, and the other side of that line can be a frightening place where children's behaviour is judged so disturbed that I've not much doubt Joe would have spiralled into hell. Instead he is accepted by staff whose generosity of spirit is overwhelming, their reserves of patience and compassion heroic. To anyone who has ever contemplated voluntary work or work with the disabled but feels it doesn't quite earn the acclaim of the world, doesn't quite measure up against their cutting and thrusting contemporaries, think of the immensity of the weight it lifts from those of us well on the way to delirium at the loneliness of care, and the richness it brings to the lives of those as dependent as Joe. The prospects for many autistic children are ghastly; Joe's now far better.

The medical prospects, though, haven't budged, and we are still very far from understanding autism. Some progress has come as a result of brain imaging in identifying areas that light up differently, some from identifying implicated genes, but at the moment this is of academic curiosity, the kind of science that will be bountiful one day, a day that comes closer, but yields modest practical benefit for the time being.

The latest theory to cause a stir – again from the agile mind of Simon Baron-Cohen and his team at Cambridge – is that autism is an extreme version of the male brain. My own view is that it's just possible there's something in this. Males are far more likely to be autistic. Of course, haemophilia is also a male problem and we don't say those who have haemophilia are extreme versions of the male. Statistical incidence is no proof of such a hypothesis. Furthermore, the theory would suggest that we should see a lower ratio of male to female cases of Asperger's, typically characterised as mild autism, and more males to females at the severe end of the spectrum. In fact, the male–female ratio is even higher in 'mild' Asperger's than it is in 'severe' autism. If the theory is correct, it might be necessary to re-characterise Asperger's as pure autism rather than mild autism and the shape of the spectrum will have to be redrawn.

Baron-Cohen's ideas hinge more critically on a typology of male and female brains as systemisers and empathisers. Empathising is 'the drive to identify another person's emotions and thoughts, and to respond to them with an appropriate emotion'. Not just the low-grade mind-reading we've talked about earlier, in other words, but caring too. Systemising is 'the drive to analyse, explore and construct a system'. The systemiser, he says, 'intuitively figures out how things work, or extracts the underlying rules that govern the behaviour of the system.' According to this theory, people with autism are strong on systemising and weak on empathising.

A fascinating current in these ideas is the tendency to talk about difference rather than deficit ('deficit is neurology's favourite word' – Oliver Sacks). This is a great leap in attitude that builds on Uta Frith's idea that some aspects of autism are a matter of cognitive style and is as big an innovation as there's been in sixty years of autism study; long overdue, in the view of some campaigners who resist talk of a cure for autism.

Yet Simon Baron-Cohen's systemising and empathising definitions are, in my view, extremely tricky to uphold with the neatness he claims, even if, as he emphasises, he's talking about men and women on average not about every single man or woman. Let's be clear, this is an order of magnitude more intelligent than any 'Mars/Venus whimsy', as one reviewer put it, but it still depends on a bipolar classification of all thought and behaviour. I'm not convinced by his bold assertion that 'systemizing and empathizing are wholly different kinds of process' with one applying uniquely to the way we understand people and the other to everything else. Take just the question of rule-building which is supposed to typify systemisers. It seems to me that our experience of life leads to a kind of rule building which applies in spades to human interaction. We learn, for example, that when Great Aunt Doris goes silent at mealtimes, you're for it, and we know this not from instinct but the clip round the ear we got last time. We apply this rule to her but not to others, though we may also use it to enrich our sense of what human silence might imply. Thus we use systemising skills to become more empathetic. Maybe thinking so proves I'm a bit autistic, but I think Baron-Cohen has more work to do on the theory yet. However, problems defining the difference between brain types don't mean there isn't one, and I suspect he will make progress.

But who am I to say? Uta Frith has written: 'The riddle of the beautiful child with autism locked in his or her own world is an irresistible challenge to amateur psychologists. They are tempted to base their answers on a few facts and observations.' Weird and wonderful speculation will flourish, she says. In the six months I've been writing this book, indulging my own weird and wonderful speculation, I've doubted my every word about Joe's disability. The enigma, as Frith calls autism, seems to float a clear deficit into view inviting a straight-forward theory, and then just when you think you have one brings to your attention an endless stream of confounding irregularities. To say Joe's disability lacks neatness would be a gross understatement. Even as I describe his lack of aware-ness of the minds of others, I recall the way he has of holding my head and looking deep into my eyes that seems to mock my understanding and hint that this is a game of deception he knows he's winning, a game he plays with infinitely more sophistication. Though he is plainly sometimes vulnerable to sensory overload, he will now and then turn on all the lights in daytime, the TV, and play on top of it all at full volume a cassette tape of Winnie the Pooh favourite songs, to which he sings along and throws himself about. Where's the sensitivity in that?

That uncertainty is a virtue in this respect was brought home to me when I came across WrongPlanet.net, a website run from the US by a group of Aspies, as they refer to them-selves. It features a satirical discussion of the problems of what they call NTs, or the neurologically typical; that's you and me, by the way.

Neurotypical syndrome is a neurobiological disorder characterized by preoccupation with social concerns, delusions of superiority, and obsession with conformity.

Neurotypical individuals often assume that their experience of the world is either the only one, or the only correct one. NTs find it difficult to be alone. NTs are often intolerant of seemingly minor differences in others.

When in groups NTs are socially and behaviorally rigid, and frequently insist upon the performance of dysfunctional, destructive, and even impossible rituals as a way of maintaining group identity.

NTs find it difficult to communicate directly, and have a much higher incidence of lying as compared to persons on the autistic spectrum.

NT is believed to be genetic in origin. Autopsies have shown the brain of the neurotypical is typically smaller than that of an autistic individual and may have over-developed areas related to social behavior.

Touché. It's not at all obvious that all characteristics of autism are for the bad. I would still insist that there are aspects of Joe I'd happily be rid of, and could imagine stripping them out without harming the essential Joe left behind. Charlotte Moore, who has written about her two autistic sons, says you can't separate the child from the autism. I disagree. I find it easy to picture a Joe who didn't hit himself, who wondered what roasted vegetable pasta parcels tasted like, instead of spinach, just for a change. I don't think I'd feel we'd lost his essence – far from it, I think we'd see him more clearly.

But I also readily accept that not everything strange is regrettable. My argument that Joe shows us by the skills he lacks what it is to be a full human being has to be tempered with the knowledge that fullness would have to include everyone, embracing all our contradictory extremes. I believe that we do not even know what we are unless we have others, different others and similar others, with whom we can compare ourselves. We are all partial, and autism, even if a little more partial than most, also adds something precious.

On holiday with Joe, his sister Cait and her best friend Ria, we arranged a game of badminton. At first Cait and Ria played while Joe and I sat and watched, but soon Joe wanted to join in. So Cait and Ria lined up on one side and Joe and I stepped onto the other. I stood behind him and helped him swing his racket in a more hopeful direction with at least some proximity to the shuttlecock.

We were soon losing badly, with less mobility around the court than a pantomime horse. And then, as a shot fell our way, we connected with it beautifully and its flight was a graceful, timeless arc of triumph beyond the reach of them both.

'Yes!' I shouted. 'Joe, we did it!'

Joe dropped his racket, dim to the rules but sensing the glory, spread his arms like wings and raced off, looping round and round our side of the court in exultant, swerving celebration, uncannily like a footballer after striking the winner in the last minute of play. Where did he learn that?

'We did it, Joe, we did it!'

I chased him round, caught him up and threw him into the air. He laughed. The girls were in hysterics. Half the sports hall was watching.

And he shouted:

'Genn!'

'Genn!'

# Epilogue: Autumn 2006

Of late we've started to notice little hints that perhaps Joe is sprouting social antennae. For instance, in the playground near Joe's school a child had a tumble and cried. Joe saw her and cried too. On another occasion some of the more sociable children and a carer were throwing a ball to each other in the school garden: Joe watched them then moved into their circle and joined in. When I hear of these new interactions my heart beats a little faster. What can it mean? Is this the beginning of a radical breakthrough to awareness sometimes found in people with Aspergers, or is that just wishful thinking?

A few months after this book was first published, I was driving in the outside lane of the M25, Joe in the back, cars in their usual tired procession at about sixty-five miles an hour. Ahead, roughly two cars distant, I saw a dash of colour and movement break abruptly from the line: a car lurched, first one way then the other then smashed head-first into the central barrier.

Suddenly we were braking and veering hard, managing to pull up on the hard shoulder behind another car that had been ahead of us and closer to disaster. The physical scene was appalling: the smell of burning rubber, the driver at the wheel sitting paralysed, door open, head bowed, sobbing, the whole motorway now at a stop.

At the same moment I shifted round to Joe, to reassure him, but he was perfectly calm. More than calm, he was sublimely content, untroubled, and began to sing, to sing in that odd, rising, light and tuneful melody of his, four notes as always: 'Di di di diii!' over and over, 'di di di diii!' signifying nothing so much as complete and carefree absent-mindedness. He'd noticed the crash. He looked, briefly, casually, in the ordinary way of surveying dull scenery. He didn't think it even interesting. He waited to drive on.

In trying to make sense of Joe's reaction later, it struck me more forcefully than ever before that, in experiencing the violence and distress of that crash I had briefly entered the absurd, breathtaking world he inhabits all the time. It savagely smashed through my bored-driver expectations, broke predictability; it was simply shocking for me to witness, yet for Joe it was – how to put it – normal.

If ever I thought that by writing about Joe I would solve his enigma, I was hopelessly wrong. In fact, having written a book that tried to pin him down I have become hawk-eyed for change. I wonder if this is what the next years will be like: on the one hand, my hopeful twitch that he is tuning into human habits and human ways; on the other, contradictory evidence of Joe's unchanging resignation to a life that must seem like a daily anarchy to which he can never give human meaning, an anarchy we glimpse in a motorway smash, but which he experiences all the time, as life crashes his attention and he tunes out of the chaos.

In short, Joe seems more ambiguous than ever. There'll be no miracle, nor anything like it. And yet, there is something stubborn in me now that wasn't there before, the feeling that by peering into his autism I've learnt only the case for more uncertainty. But uncertainty cuts both ways and nowadays it just won't go away, this thought, that maybe … just maybe …

# Acknowledgements

It takes a whole village to raise a child, and Joe is no ordinary child. So to the teeming metropolis of carers, teachers, neighbours and helpful friends and relatives; the staff at Aldenham, St Margaret's and Colnebrook schools, particularly Colnebrook's head teacher Richard; the many professionals from the LEA who always got there in the end; Josie, Joanna and the team from the ABA years; Hester, Tom, Tash, Richard, Orna, Vicky, Jackie and the rest of the staff at St Christopher's school; Roger and Jean; Ron and Shirley, my endlessly supportive parents and Alan; spotty-dogs Jenny, Jessie, Paul (not least for the running) and Sue, Jo and Simon, most of the other Heathens who've tolerated Joe on the rampage through their houses or trampling their gardens, the card sharps and many others who've been part of his life before he went to school and since, giving both practical help and emotional support, several of the boys included – Adam, Ceps – little though some of them probably thought of it, I say thank you. I'm grateful to the staff at Great Ormond Street. Annika deserves special mention for years of devotion. I particularly want to thank Joe's mother, Sarah, who has put her heart into Joe, and knows what it's like. Then, of course, there's Cait, whose company, tolerance and understanding has been more precious than she can know.

For help with the book I'd like to thank colleagues at Radio 4 – Nicola Meyrick, Innes Bowen, Rosie Goldsmith – for many useful conversations, as well as Helen Boaden and Radio 4 itself for the opportunity to make a two-part programme called *Being Joe* broadcast in April 2005, and Mark Damazer for his appreciation. Many other colleagues in current-affairs radio, Smita, Sam, Zillah, Daniel, Mark, Gwyn and others too numerous to name, have been interested and encouraging, creating an atmosphere of appreciative curiosity that helped no end to make sure I was so publicly committed to getting the thing written that it couldn't be otherwise. Thanks, folks. Felipe Fernandez-Armesto threw his uniquely inquisitive intelligence at me in a way that turned my thoughts on a sixpence, and was never less than marvellous company. I'm also grateful to Simon Baron-Cohen and, for some great conversations and ideas, to Kenan Malik. Mary Colyer has been supportive and asked the right kind of difficult questions, as has Chris Vinz. Thanks too to 'Magic' from WrongPlanet.net, for his honesty and insight, and to Karen Pleskus for the example she set. My sharp and mischievous editor Andrew Franklin and his colleagues at Profile gave encouragement to the idea from the off, with an attitude of no-nonsense, responsible enthusiasm that was a breath of fresh air. More power to them. Galen Strawson was generous with his time and advice on points about consciousness, talked me out of saying some silly things about narrative selves and gave other valuable advice, with great sensitivity.

I owe a lot to Andrew Dilnot who read drafts, made typically wise and incisive observations and has been an endlessly understanding, thoughtful and moral voice throughout Joe's life. Finally, I'd like to thank Katey Adderley, who has been a joy, patient, supportive and encouraging, and who read and re-read every chapter and made numerous helpful suggestions in her customary modest and clever way. The silly things I still say are all my own.

# Further Reading

Whatever originality you find in this book is owed mostly to Joe, who has been my excuse for trespassing on other people's expertise.

For an introduction to autism the single best volume remains Uta Frith's *Autism: Explaining the Enigma* (Blackwell 2003). The subject has moved fast in recent years and Frith has been often at the forefront of new research, experiments and ideas. Her book gives historical context, useful case studies, a well-organised summary of the latest thinking and some valuable reflections on trends, therapies and prospects. Francesca Happe, who has worked extensively with Frith, offers a useful short summary of these in support of ideas about central coherence and autism which at the time of writing is available at: http://www.mindship.org/happe.htm.

Simon Baron-Cohen has been a fertile source of ideas and intuition about autism for many years and has also worked with Frith. *Mindblindness: An Essay on Autism and Theory of Mind* (MIT Press 1997) is an introduction to the ideas he helped develop and popularise which have, I suspect, made more concrete the thoughts of many parents about what's missing in their autistic children. It goes into a good deal of largely speculative detail about the pieces of mental machinery that comprise our mind-reading abilities and also suggests evolutionary explanations. But it is concerned with the mind-blindness deficit and does not explore, as Frith does, theories which account for the islets of ability in autism. Most recently, Baron-Cohen produced *The Essential Difference* (Penguin 2004), which develops his ideas, nurtured over more than ten years, that autism is an extreme version of the male (systemising) brain. This is as much a contribution to debates arising from evolutionary psychology about gender as it is to autism research and invites as many questions as it answers, but it's courageous and imaginative.

Baron-Cohen drew significantly, as I do, on Nicholas Humphrey's brilliant *Consciousness Regained* (OUP 1984), which describes our mind-reading capacity beautifully and speculates about its origins and links with self-consciousness. Humphrey describes himself as a theoretical psychologist, a pastime that leaves cold proper biologists like Steve Jones, but with an output that has continually fascinated me. Despite the acclaim his book received, Humphrey has since moved away from its central explanation of consciousness but mostly because he now defines it differently. His latest ideas can be found in *The Mind Made Flesh: Essays from the Frontiers of Psychology and Evolution* (Oxford Paperbacks, 2002) and the just-published *Seeing Red, a Study in Consciousness* (Belknap Press, 2006). Humphrey shares a great deal, when he isn't at affable loggerheads, with the philosopher Daniel Dennett, whose *The Intentional Stance* (MIT 1987) did much to define and develop the mind-reading thesis.

For those interested in questions about what makes us human, an entertaining and sceptical exploration of the definitions can be found in Felipe Fernandez-Armesto's *So You Think You're Human?* (OUP 2005), an audacious tour of the arguments. Mary Midgley is one of my favourite philosophers and her *Beast and Man: The Roots of Human Nature* (Routledge 2002) is full of humour and wisdom. John Macmurray's *Persons in Relation* (Humanity 1998) and *The Self as Agent* (Prometheus 1991) are also close to my heart. Thomas Nagel is less directly relevant but *The View From Nowhere* (OUP 1989) is a seriously clever inquiry into the problem of comparing subjective and objective perception and manages never to forget the importance of everyday experience and intuition. *Mortal Questions*, also by Nagel (Canto 1979), includes the wonderful essay 'What Is It Like to Be a Bat?', which is often referred to in discussions about understanding other states of consciousness. The best popular account of the nature/nurture row I've come across recently is Matt Ridley's *Nature Via Nurture: Genes, Experience and What Makes Us Human* (HarperCollins 2003). It's full of detail and arresting examples and has a sustained and powerful central argument which ought to bring some much-needed calm to this subject. I also particularly admire Kenan Malik's *Man Beast and Zombie: What Science Can and Cannot Tell Us about Human Nature* (Phoenix 2001), which places these arguments in a historical context to show that our idea of human nature is shaped by our wider social concerns and intellectual fashions.

On the developmental side, Paul Bloom's *Descartes' Baby:*

*How the Science of Human Development Explains What Makes Us Human* (Heinemann 2004) is a delight. It combines philosophy and developmental psychology with references ranging from literature to modern art and neuroscience to make the arresting case that we are all instinctive dualists. It describes much else besides about what babies know, all with an enviable lightness of touch. I have to mention Margaret Donaldson's *Children's Minds* (HarperCollins 1986), part educational polemic, part developmental psychology; it is elegantly argued, a persuasive attack on Piaget and still relevant, I think. As a general reference work and bibliography on child development, I also used *Understanding Children's Development* by Peter Smith, Helen Cowie and Mark Blades (Blackwell 2003). It's not written with verve exactly, but is clear, balanced, thoughtful and covers the ground. Francis Spufford's *The Child that Books Built* (Faber & Faber 2003) is a richly intelligent assemblage of memoir, developmental psychology and philosophy that particularly influenced my chapter on storytelling.

Among autobiographies, Temple Grandin's *Emergence: Labelled Autistic* (Time Warner International 1996) is the most well known and a fascinating read, but so extraordinary is she that it is not perhaps typical. But then, the typical may never be written. Her more recent *Animals in Translation: Using the Mysteries of Autism to Decode Animal Behaviour* (Bloomsbury 2005) came out in the UK just as I was finishing this and would certainly have been a stronger influence if I'd discovered it earlier. Lately, I've found the exchanges on a website for those with

Asperger's syndrome, http://www.WrongPlanet.net/, absolutely captivating, written with honesty and great intelligence.

I am reluctant to recommend books that offer cures or therapies for autism. Some I find implausible, others more reasonable but still often far too hopeful and tending to claim too much understanding with too much certainty. Too many, in my view, are also published in support of therapeutic regimes available exclusively through some specialist network of instructors which often cost a great deal of money. This is not to claim that they are useless – we have found aspects of them helpful and others have reported impressive results – but they do not suit everyone equally. There's a desperate need for some thorough, independent evaluation of their claims and methods.

For those seeking general advice about what to do if they suspect their child has autism or who have other general inquiries, the National Autistic Society offers a helpline and much excellent advice and support: http://www.nas.org.uk/ or 0845 070 4004.